INTRODUCTION TO NANOTECHNOLOGY

SYNTHESIS, CHARACTERIZATION, AND APPLICATIONS OF NANOPARTICLES

ASHOK KUMAR

Made with ♥ on the Notion Press Platform
www.notionpress.com

Dedicated to:-

"My Parents"

for

"raising me to believe that anything is possible"

Contents

Preface

Nanotechnology is the creation of materials, components, devices, and systems at the near-atomic or nanometer level, "Nano" means one-billionth. Nanotechnology is creating manufacturing possibilities, which in turn will profoundly impact our economy, our environment, and our society. Nanotechnology is the technological advances that rely on the properties of products at a very tiny scale. In nanotechnology, a 100 nm dimension is essential, as under this limit we can carefully examine the new properties of matter. At present, nanotechnology is a subject, on which research and study are going on a large scale. Nanotechnology is in its infancy never the less the potential to rearrange the matter on an atomic is known and due to our enhancing ability to fabricate and characterize feature sizes below a hundred nm, a lot of products are there on the market. It is due to nanotechnology that today we can produce many new products and devices having many uses like in medicine, electronics, energy production, etc. many issues of concern are being raised by nanotechnology.

Chapter 1 *starts with an introduction to nanotechnology. This chapter also tells the history of nanotechnology and also highlights its uses.*

Chapter 2 *discusses the fundamental concept and approaches of nanotechnology. It deals with top-down and bottom-up approaches to nanotechnology. The discussion on the approaches is followed by molecular nanotechnology.*

Chapter 3 *tells the nanoparticles and their properties. It also discusses the characterization of nanoparticles.*

Chapter 4 *introduces the nanomaterials along with diamond, graphite, fullerene, and also carbon nanotubes. Their properties and applications are also discussed.*

Chapter 5 *tells the various applications of nanotechnology. The applications in various fields increase the importance of nanotechnology.*

Chapter 6 *is devoted to the impacts of nanotechnology. It also discusses the health and safety impacts, and societal impacts of nanotechnology.*

Chapter 7 *starts with the advantages of nanotechnology. This chapter also deals with the disadvantages of nanotechnology.*

Chapter 8 *provides suggestions for the future.*

Acknowledgements

I wish to express my heartful gratitude to my father **Mr. Manveer Singh** *and my mother* **Mrs. Bimala Devi.**

I thankfully acknowledge the support of my sister **Mrs. SumanSangwan** *and my brother-in-law* **Mr. Ashok Sangwan.**

Also thanks to **Mr. Ishwar Singh Karwasara** *&* **Mr.Vidhyadhar Karwasara** *for giving suggestions and friendly advice during my work.*

Without the help of my cousin **Satish Choudhary**, *this work would have been an uphill task.*

I affectionately quote my feelings for my Grandparents **Mr. Manfool Singh Dangi** *&* **Mrs. Hoshiyari Devi, Mr. Partap Singh Karwasara** *&* **Mrs. Giniya Devi,** *and my family members who always showered their blessings and affections on me, which enabled me to complete this work. I bow my head towards them.*

I express my heart-touching and warm feelings to my friends and colleagues who gave enthusiastic moral support and inspiration.

In the very last but not least, I thank the Almighty God for giving me the strength and perseverance to complete this task.

CHAPTER I

INTRODUCTION TO NANOTECHNOLOGY

Introduction:-

Nanotechnology, also called "nanotech," is the study of matter that is controlled at the molecular and atomic scale. Materials made by exploiting natural resources consist of atoms. The arrangement of atoms forms the basis for the properties of those products. Computer chips can also be made by rearranging the atoms. Similarly, we can make potatoes by rearranging the atoms in water, air, and dirt. Nanotechnology refers to technological advances based on the properties of products on a very small scale. In nanotechnology, a 100-nanometer dimension is essential, as under this limit we can carefully examine the new properties of matter. At the moment, nanotechnology is the subject of extensive research and investigation. It has improved many aspects of life, including cleaner, faster, and safer manufacturing reduced the use of harmful resources, and extended product life cycles. Although nanotechnology is still in its infancy, the potential to rearrange matter on an atomic scale is known, and many products are available on the market as a result of our improving ability to fabricate and characterize feature sizes below 100 nm.

It is due to nanotechnology that today we can produce many new products and devices with many uses, like in medicine, electronics, energy production, etc. Many issues of concern are being raised by nanotechnology. These issues are about the environmental influence and toxicity of nanomaterials and their impacts on global economics, involving the speculation of many doomsday scenarios. Nanoscience is the study of the nanoscale intersection of disciplines such as biology, physics, chemistry, engineering, computer science, and so on. Due to the provision of more funds and the advancement of nanotechnology, its centers are opening all around the world.

The appearance of the word "nanotechnology" is increasing in scientific journals and the news. The nanotechnology industry faced a great shift from its hype stage to the commercialization stage. Many surveys have been conducted in the U.S. manufacturing industry, which points out that 58% of the 600 respondents will have products manufactured by nanotechnology within the next 3 years. This study has been conducted by the National Center for Manufacturing Sciences (NCMS). The top products include semiconductors, which have properties between conductors and insulators (e.g., germanium), nanowires, coatings, thin films, etc. These products are available on the market.

Nanotechnology is a very transformative technology due to its known effects on the steam engine of the 19th century, the electricity of the 20th century, and the internet in contemporary society. Nature has proven to be a master at nanoscale operations. It has always relied on these operations for the functioning of life, for example, the metabolic activities within cells for sustaining life and the fertilization of an embryo in the reproduction of cellular components for cell movement.

The natural system called the "ecosystem" is also dependent on nanotechnology. For the rain and snow, then, formation is dependent on nanoparticles. Raindrops are formed by the condensation of small airborne particles. Depending on the temperature, the particles can vary in size from 1000 nm to 100 nm or even less. Dust, volcanoes, forest or factory smoke, phytoplankton, or ocean salt can lead to the emergence of nanoparticles. In today's world, nanotechnology is very important as it involves little effort, labor, land, or maintenance. It is considered essential because of its high productivity. It is also not very costly and needs only a small amount of materials and energy. one of the bases of major economic revolutions. At the start, GPTs were known to have limited uses, but with time, they spread into new applications. Investors should be optimistic about the continuity and acceleration of creative destruction, which will put nanotechnology at its core.

Definition of nanotechnology:-

In reality, utilizing present tools and technologies, nanotechnology is projected to make items from the bottom up so that high-performance products can be produced. At an atomic scale, nanotechnology is the engineering of functional systems.

In 1980, nanotechnology was popularised by K. Eric Drexler. He then discussed the formation of machines on a molecular scale, robot arms, nanometer-wide motors, and computers. In the coming 10 years, he will describe and analyze these unbelievable devices and respond to the accusations of science fiction. The National Nanotechnology Initiative (NNI) was formed in the United States to fund this field of nanotechnology, and by their definition, nanotechnology is always less than 1000 nm in size and has novel great properties.

Most of the work and labor that is done in the name of nanotechnology is not that in the small sense; the meaning of nanotechnology is making things like buildings that start from the bottom up with atomic precision. This theory was envisioned by the famous physicist Richard Feynman in 1959.

Many definitions are concerned with the control and study of phenomena and products with sizes of about 100 nm and compare them to human hair that is 80,000 nm wide. On the one hand, definitions of nanotechnology involve a reference to molecular systems, while nanotechnology purists say that references to functional systems must be included in many definitions of nanotechnology. In the first issue of Nature Technology, 13 researchers were asked to define "nanotechnology," and their responses reflect a range of viewpoints. The size limitations of nanotechnology seem to be in the 1-100 nm range. Many experts caution against a hard definition based on sub-100 nm sizes. The most important requirement for the definition of nanotechnology is the special properties of nanostructures, which are due to their nanoscale proportions.

Guided by molecular machine systems, advanced technology will use positionally controlled mechanical chemistry. This was by the plan to use nanomachines in miniature factories to construct complex products. Another important criterion for the definition is the requirement that nanostructures be manmade. The development of a nanotechnology roadmap is one of the goals of the Battelle-led broad-based technology roadmap project. This project is also led by the Foresight Nanotech Institute (FNI). The manager of many United States national laboratories is Battelle.

Generations of nanotechnology:-

Michael Rocco of the United States National Nanotechnology Initiative represented four generations of nanotechnology development. Based on the products that resulted and came up, nanotechnology's evolution can be divided into four generations. According to Rocco, nanotechnology's first generation started in the year 2000. Passive nanostructures are the names given to all first-generation products that must perform a single function, such as aerosols and colloids. Second-generation products are called active nanostructures, and they started in 2005. They must perform a variety of functions, including acting as actuators and sensors. The third generation began in 2010. It is considered the era of systems based on nanosystems. In these nanosystems, many interacting elements are included, such as robotics, guided assembly, 3D networking, etc. In 2015, the fourth generation of nanotechnology will emerge. In that year, it is expected that the first integrated nanosystems will develop.

Nanotechnology has a promising future. When compared to competing products, its applications are also very impressive. So speculation about nanotechnology's future may be very amusing and interesting. The engineering of functional systems at the molecular scale is included in the basic definition of nanotechnology. In almost all major fields of the industrial and secondary sectors, nanotechnology has widely spread. Many experts believe that nanotechnology is the measurement or visualization of the 100 nm scale, but the ability to control and restructure matter at the atomic scale is a significant element. If more work is done in the next four generations that leads to molecular nanosystems that involve molecular manufacturing, then it can be said that nanotech is really about the engineering of functional systems at the nanoscale.

The development of nanotechnology reveals the fact that the products that seem impossible today will become possible with the advancement and development of nanotechnology, and the field of electronics will also progress. Poor dissipation and contamination of particles are the major issues of concern today, which are hazards to us. These risks can be avoided by utilizing ultra-high-purity products and cutting-edge technologies. Using these techniques, we can even produce smaller computer chips with higher speeds and miniaturized electronic products. By using traditional methods, the production of capacitors with amazing capacitance is unimaginable. But the use of nanomaterials has made it possible.

It is only due to nanotechnology that we will be able to buy rapid computers, tiny mobile devices, and other small electronic devices in the coming time. Nanotechnology is called "general-purpose technology" (GPT) due to its effects on almost all industries and society. In every field and aspect of life, nanotechnology will prove successful. It will provide us with better-built, longer-lasting, cleaner, safer, and smarter materials that are good for homes, communications, medicine, agriculture, transportation, industry, etc. It will provide efficiency in almost every aspect of life. We can't say that nanotechnology provides only better products. On the other hand, it also provides an improved manufacturing process. As a GPT, nanotechnology will be useful for commercial purposes and also in the military, where it will provide a great helping hand by making many powerful weapons and tools. A large number of copies of data files can be made by the computer at little or no cost. What we need is for product development to become as inexpensive as copying a file. This is the real meaning of nanotechnology, and that's why it is seen as the next industrial revolution. Along with miniature chemical processes, computing and robotics enable a wide range of items to be made quickly, cleanly, and inexpensively; products can also be made directly from blueprints.

History of nanotechnology:-

Humans were previously unaware of nanotechnology, but it was still used to make steel, paintings, and rubber through vulcanization. The atomic ensembles used for all these processes were more than 1000 nanometers in size from the base. We know that for 1000 years, pottery that uses nano-sized particles has been in use. The oldest object known to have been made from pottery is expected to be the "Lycurgus Chalice," which can be found in the British Museum and dates back to the late fourth century A.D.

The raised frieze on the Roman chalice depicts the myth of king Lycurgus. The glass in this appears clear when viewed directly, but green when viewed in reflected light. The extraordinary and uncommon effect is due to the presence of about 70 nm of silver and gold particles in the glass. This may be possible due to the addition of some scrap metal and slag containing silver and gold when the glass was being made. The credit for the discovery that glass can be colored red by adding a small amount of gold is given to Johann Kunkel of Germany, who worked on this in the late 17th century.

The use of nanoparticles in ancient times is not limited to chalice. Pottery from the 9th century A.D. from the Mesopotamian era also has nanoparticles contained in it. Due to the spread of Arabian culture, this technology was introduced to Spain, and then it was brought to Italy. We have an enormous space for the storage of information. Richard Feynman delivered a lecture in 1959 that was entitled, "There is plenty of room at the bottom." It is said in the speech that it is our clumsy size that manipulates the single molecules of atoms, as they are very tiny for our tools, which are considered to be fully theoretical and seem to be fantastic. He explained that the law described in physics doesn't restrict our ability to manipulate atoms and molecules and doesn't prevent us from doing so.

We don't have appropriate ways of doing this. He predicted that the time at which manipulation of matter will be possible will come. He was correct, or accurate, in assuming this. We were accustomed to the top-down approach, but Prof. Feynman described and explained the bottom-up approach. We developed and discovered numerous methods by which Prof. Feynman's discoveries and findings were validated. Professor Feynman described scanning probe microscopy as one of his most famous methods. Prof. Feynman predicted that single atoms and molecules would be positioned in the desired place by scanning probe microscopy (SPM), and this has proved to be true.

Pre-18th Century:

Roman Period (30 BC–640 AD):

Nanotechnology materials were in use in ancient times. The clues for this use have been taken from archaeological remains. The Lycurgus cup, the famous artifact of this period, can be seen in the British Museum in London. Its base is made of glass and dates back to the fourth century, and the specialty of this cup is due to its color-changing property from green to red. It has been found that the glass consists of nanoparticles of silver and gold. The properties of materials at the nanoscale are completely different from those of their macroscale counterparts.

Medieval Period (500–1450 AD):

The standard glass appears red due to the presence of gold nanoparticles present in the glass matrix, while the deep yellow color is due to silver nanoparticles. The size of the metal nanoparticles produced these color variations. This example of the dramatic change in material properties at the nanoscale is a key component of nanotechnology.

Renaissance Period (1450–1600 AD):

Discoveries in nanotechnology were also practiced by Deruta Umbria in the fifteenth and sixteenth centuries. Deruta's products, such as dramatic indecent or metallic glazes, were in high demand in Europe during the fifteenth and sixteenth centuries. Copper and silver metal particles ranging in size from 5 to 100 billionths of a meter were used to achieve the red and gold luster effects. Copper and silver particles did not make the light scatter. Instead, they cause the light to bounce off of the thin surface and also at different wavelengths, which produces metallic and iridescent effects. During the same period in India, many artisans created wonderful objects based on nanotechnology that are now in the Jodhpur, Udaipur, and Bundi museums.

Pre-19th Century:

1827 (Photography):-

Photography, which depends on silver nanoparticle production, is an early example of nanotechnology. Transparent cellulose acetate forms the base of photographic film, which is coated with a thin layer of gelatin consisting of silver halides. Silver halides are decomposed by the light produced by silver nanoparticles, which are considered pixels in a photographic image.

In the 13th century, images were produced using silver nitrate and chloride by the British scientists Thomas Wedgewood and Sir Humphrey Dray, but their images were temporary. With the use of material that gets hardened when exposed to light, Joseph Niepce produced the first successful photograph in 1827. But this picture required an eight-hour exposure to light. Niepce and another scientist, Louse Daguerre, worked together on photography, but after four years, Niepce died from a stroke, and Daguerre continued to experiment. Finally, in 1839, he became successful, and a way of developing photographic plates was discovered. The light exposure time was reduced from 8 hours to

12 hours per hour. It has also been discovered that the image can be made permanent by immersing it in salt.

1857 (Discovery of Gold Colloids):

In 1856, Michael Faraday prepared and discovered metallic colloids, even though the word "nano" was not in use at that time. Colloid particles are very fine, and they suspend in a solution. Colloidal particles can't be seen with the naked eye. Their size is between those particles that dissolve in solution and those that settle down. There were many properties in the gold colloids, such as those of electronics and optics.

Faraday, an English chemist, and physicist received a little more education than primary education. He began using a bookbinder when he was 14 years old. His interest in physical and chemical terms started to develop there. He also sent the notes he took after listening to his lectures to the famous chemist Humphrey Davy, who hired him as an assistant in the laboratory of a royal institution in London when he was 21 years old. The specimens that Faraday used for his research in 1856 are found at the Royal Institution of Great Britain. In 1867, Faraday thought of an experiment that was popularly known as Maxwell's Demon. It has the potential to handle individual molecules. It was then that the distinct concepts of nanotechnology were first described.

Pre-20th Century:-

The first observations and size calculations of nanoparticles were made or described in the twentieth century. These discoveries happened due to the efforts of Richard Adolf Zsigmondy, who studied gold and other nanomaterials having a size range of ten nm and less. A book published by Richard Adolf Zsigmondy was released in 1914. Zsigmondy used the first nanometer to characterize particle size. Zsigmondy defined one nanometer as 1/1,000,000 nm. The first system of classification was developed by him and depended on particle size in the nanometer range. In the area of colloid science and interfaces, many important developments occurred in the 20th century.

The nanolayer, a layer of material one molecule thick, was introduced by Irving Langmuir and Katharine B. Blodgett. Langmuir was also awarded the Nobel Prize in Chemistry for his work and contributions to nanotechnology. The first measurements of forces were conducted by Derjaguin and Abrikosova in the early 1950s. On the periodic colloid principles and structures of molecular self-assembly, many studies have been conducted, and modern nanotechnology depends on many inventions and discoveries. The topic on modern technology, "Fundamentals of Interface and Colloid Science," was given by J. Lyklema.

On Dec. 29, 1959, at the American Physical Society meeting at Caltech, the topic of nanotechnology was again taken up by Richard Feynman, who delivered a popular lecture entitled "There is plenty of room at the bottom." This idea seems easily acceptable, and it is also enhanced by exponential assembly with parallelism so that a useful quantity of end products can be produced. Two challenges were declared by Feynman at a meeting, and the first individual to solve each one would get a prize of $1000. William McLellan completed the first challenge, which was the construction of the nanometer, in November 1960. Another challenge was the possibility of scanning down letters, so Tom Newman won the prize for Encyclopedia Britannica in 1985. Gordon Moore made the observation known as Moore's law in 1965 when the silicon transition was continuously scanning downward.

1908 (MIE Theory):

With his theory of light scattering by particles, Gustav Mie (a German physicist) played a significant role in the development of nanotechnology. It was illustrated by his theory that short-wavelength light is scattered more effectively from the particles as compared to long-wavelength light. For instance, the sky is seen as blue because particles of air scatter the blue light from the sun more effectively than yellow or red. After all, it has a shorter wavelength than yellow or red light.

Dust particles also contribute to the scattering of light. When the sun sets, it travels farther through the atmosphere than it does when it rises. The color that is seen is determined by the size of the particles. The MIE theory helped scientists realize this. A method or way was devised by MIE theory for calculating the size of particles and the amount of light scattered by particles. This theory requires large numbers of calculations for larger particles and nanoparticles. Twenty years earlier, when supercomputers were available, this theory was rarely used. The size of nanoparticles is determined and predicted by the researchers through the MIET theory.

1931 (Electron Microscope):

In 1931, during the Renaissance period, light microscopes were used to see things, but they did not get recognition as they were not suitable for seeing things smaller than the wavelength of visible light. A new and small world will be opened by a new microscope called the electron microscope, which was the result of the partnership of German scientists Max Knott and Ernest Ruska. In a new and small world with this microscope, electrons are made to accelerate in a vacuum, so that their wavelength can be made even shorter—only one hundred thousandth that of white light. The clarity and details of a conventional light microscope were exceeded by the electron microscope in 1993. This was an essential step for developing those instruments and techniques that would enable research at the nanoscale.

1947 (The Transistor):

Until the mid-1940s, the state of the art in electronics was vacuum tubes. Their use was widespread. Because they can change direct currents and amplify an electron signal, they were used to power the first high-speed computers and telephone calls. More tubes were needed for making powerful computers, and these tubes were difficult to carry and were large and heavy too. These tubes were easily breakable, and they overheat easily. A research group to look into finding a solution was established by Bell Labs in 1945. Williams Shockley was the leader of this group, and Walter Brattain and John Bardeen were also in the group.

With the use of the germanium element, Braden and Bratton created an amplifying circuit. It was called a "point contact transistor" by them, but until Shockley impoverished the original idea with a junction transistor in 1951, the discovery did not gain attention. The electrical properties of transistors are similar to those of vacuum tubes, but they are less expensive. It was small and consumed little power continuously. The three men shared the 1956 Nobel Prize in Physics "for their research on semiconductors and their discovery of the transistor effect." The invention of the transistor and the integrated circuit marked the beginning of microelectronics, a field that relies on tools for miniaturization. The semiconductor industry is one of the largest technology drivers in the field of nanotechnology. Researchers today are looking to enable the creation of chips holding billions or even trillions of nanoscale transistors.

1951 (Field-ion electron microscope):

Erwin Muller, a professor at Penn State University, invented the field ion electron microscope in 1951. Individual atoms and their arrangements could be viewed for the first time in history. For this accomplishment, Professor Mueller is known as the first person to "see" atoms.

1953 (discovery of DNA):

The discovery of DNA was one of the twentieth century's most significant events. Scientists knew by the 1950s that DNA (deoxyribonucleic acid) was the carrier of genetic information, but its workings and structure were unknown. DNA was published by Dr. James Watson and Prof. Francis Crick in 1953. They discovered that after cell division, the two strands of the DNA helix separate, and a new "other half" is formed on each strand. It stated that DNA reproduction by itself is possible. After many decades, the ability of DNA to assemble itself into small structures would be an inspiration for researchers to use the same principle to develop nanoscale structures with specific dimensions and chemical properties.

1958 (Tunneling Phenomenon):

In 1958, Leo Esaki, a Japanese physicist working at Sony Corporation, discovered that electrons could sometimes "tunnel" through a potential barrier formed at the junctions of certain semiconductors, even though classical theory predicted that this was not possible. What Dr. Esaki's observations tell us about the control of materials at the nanoscale by separate and different laws of behavior is that they are controlled by quantum mechanics as opposed to classical physics. The discovery resulted in the development of the tunneling diode (also known as the Esaki diode), an important component of solid-state physics, as well as the first time tunneling (a key nano-electronics phenomenon), was used in a real device.

1959 (Richard Feynman):

Richard Feynman, who won the Nobel Prize in physics, predicted the possibilities and potentials of tiny materials. Electric motors and the size of our little fingers nails were also discussed. There is also a device on the market that allows the Lord's Prayer to be written on the head of the pin. When they look back in 2000 at this stage, they will wonder why nobody began seriously moving in this direction until the year 1960.

1960 (Ferro-fluids):-

In the 1960s, NASA researchers were trying to find ways to control liquids in space. They discovered that nano-sized magnetic particles of iron that were given a chemical coating or surfactant that prevented them from clumping together could be dispersed in oil or water. They could then control the location of the fluid (called a ferrofluid) with a magnet. On Earth, ferrofluids are used inside loudspeakers, where they help keep the inner parts cool. They are also used on computer hard drives and in semiconductor manufacturing as seals to keep out dust and other contaminants. Nanotechnology wants to harness ferrofluids for other important uses, such as developing tiny sensors or placing them inside the body as biomedical devices to deliver drugs, absorb toxins, or provide hypothermia. It is even possible that ferrofluids could be used to help clean up hazardous waste spills.

1960 (Zeolite Catalysts):

Zeolites are amorphous materials that are derived from non-living things. It works like molecular silver, which allows some molecules to pass through it but restricts or breaks others. Their discovery and invention are still going on. They can be either synthetic (man-made) or natural. For making chemical reactions fast, Charles Plank and Edward Rosinski developed a new process to use these in 1960. Their focus was on the use of zeolites for breaking petroleum into gasoline more rapidly and efficiently.

At present, researchers are trying hard to design a Zeolite catalyst at the nanoscale by controlling the size and shapes of molecules that can enter. If the process of producing gasoline from petroleum becomes successful, then we will get more and cleaner gasoline from every barrel of oil. It is expected by the researchers that the cost and pollution related to the production of many petroleum products, including gasoline, would be reduced by nanotechnology.

1965 (Moore's Law):

It has been noted by the founder of Intel Corporation that the number of transistors per integrated circuit has doubled every two years. He predicted that this trend would continue for the next 10 years, and his prediction was quickly dubbed "Moore's law" by the press. Moore's prediction turned out to be prophetic. In reality, long after 1975, the complexity of a chip continued to double every year. The rate of doubling has only recently slowed to about every 18 months. Many researchers believe that these devices, which use electronics, nanotechnology, and molecular electronics, will keep Moore's law accurate and correct.

1970 (Sir John Pole's Software):

Developing new mathematical formulas is an essential part of science, and as science becomes more complicated, new, faster formulas are needed. Although computers had become significantly more powerful by this point, new software was required to make that power useful. Up until this time, it was very difficult to solve the complex mathematical equations needed to determine the properties of molecules. In 1970, John Pole and his research group developed Gaussian, a software program that would perform these calculations. This pioneer in the use of computers to assume the behavior of atoms and molecules also developed many of the algorithms that made computer-based modeling at the nanoscale possible.

1974 (First Use of the Term "Nanotechnology"):

In his 1974 paper, Norio Taniguchi of Tokyo Science University defined nanotechnology as follows: Nanotechnology is the branch of science that deals with the process of separation, consolidation, and deformation of materials by one atom's worth of molecules. Nanotechnology's definition has evolved. Many new concepts have been added to these mechanical aspects, like quantum dots, which were also enhanced by nanotech. "Nanotechnology" is defined as technology involving characteristics or features smaller than 100 nm.

1974 (Molecular Electronics):

In 1974, Mark A. Ratner of Northwestern University and A. Aviram of IBM proposed that the behavior of basic electronic devices was exhibited by individual molecules, allowing computers to be built from the ground up by transforming individual molecules into circuit components. This application of nanotechnology was so typical that it was formulated before the means and ways that came up later to check and test it. It was so radical that it was not continued or understood widely for another 15 years. For this groundbreaking work, Ratner is also known as the "Father of Molecular Scale Electronics".

1977 (Surface Enhanced Raman Spectroscopy):

In nanotechnology, the required tools have been in the making for many years. For example, spectroscopy is a set of techniques that use the interaction of light with matter to obtain information about its density and the structure of its molecules. Sir Raman won the Nobel Prize in Physics in 1920 for his discovery that light scattered by molecules could be used to give information about the composition and molecular structure of a chemical sample. Despite being a groundbreaking technique, Raman spectroscopy cannot detect at the nanoscale.

The technique was greatly improved in the 1960s by the invention of the laser, but it was not until 1977 when Richard P. Dyne discovered Surface Enhanced Raman Spectroscopy (SERS), that nanoscale studies became possible. Van Dyne deduced that Raman intensity would be amplified 1,000 times if molecules were attached to the surface, which had hills and 50-100 nm-sized valleys. The discovery of SERS completely transformed Raman spectroscopy from one of the least sensitive techniques to one of the most sensitive techniques in all of the molecular spectroscopy. Today, SERS is used to study the chemical reactions of molecules in electrochemistry, catalysis, materials synthesis, and biochemistry. The sensitivity of SERS is now so high that even single molecules can be studied.

1980 (Self-Assembled Monolayers):

In 1980, Jacob Sagiv at the Weitzman Institute in Israel discovered that molecules containing a chemical called octadecyl trichlorosilane, or OTS, would spontaneously react with a glass surface to self-assemble into individual layers. In 1983, a Bell Labs research team led by David Allara discovered that molecules with thiol groups (groups containing sulfur) on a gold surface would also self-assemble into individual or nanolayers. These self-assembled monolayers are typically a few nanometers thick (determined by the choice of the molecule) and allow researchers to tailor the properties of a surface. For the first time, scientists could envision building three-dimensional nanoscale structures layer by layer. These structures are being used to build molecule-based electronic devices, biosensors, and new types of optical materials.

1981 (Scanning Tunneling Microscope):

Gerd Binning and Heinrich Rohr discovered STM in 1981 at the IBM Research Laboratory in Zurich, Switzerland. This invention allowed scientists to not only observe nanoscale particles, atoms, and small molecules but to control them. Between the tip of the probe and the surface, the surface of the sample is scanned by STM. As the electricity begins to flow, the STM can determine minute variations in the distance electrons travel. In this way, the STM maps the surface of the sample. The information is saved in a data file, and a "picture" of the surface is created by the computer. In this way, the STM can "see" atomic-scale objects. The STM helps researchers determine the size and form of molecules, observe defects and abnormalities, and discover how chemicals interact with the sample. The STM quickly became standard equipment in laboratories throughout the world.

1985 (the "Buckyball"):

C60, which is a structure of carbon nanoparticles shaped like a soccer ball, was discovered by Richard Smalley, Robert Curl, and graduate student James Health at Rice University, along with Sir Harry Kroto of Sussex University. This resulted in the breakthrough of another nanotechnology in 1985. Buckminster Fullerene is a molecule named after the visionary American architect and engineer Buckminster Fuller. More commonly called a "buckyball," the molecule is extremely rugged and capable of surviving collisions with metals and other materials at speeds higher than 20,000 miles per hour. Because of this ruggedness, buckyballs show promise in the development of fuel cells that might power the automobiles of the future. Researchers are also investigating the possibility of using buckyballs as tiny drug delivery systems.

1986 (Atomic Force Microscope):

Greg Binning and his colleague Christoph Gerber invented the atomic force microscope at IBM. It was to study a surface directly, in the same way that a record is studied by a record player. An atom-by-atom topographical map is created by measuring the atomic forces that exert a pull on the cantilever. 3-D images of an object's surface are created by AFM with extremely high magnifications.

1987 (Single-Electron Tunneling Transistor):

Scientists Dmitri Averring and Konstantin Likharev developed and prepared a new device known as an "electron tunneling transistor." These scientists were working at Moscow University. It happened in 1985, and after two years, the device was made by Theodore Fulton and Gerald Dolan at Bell Labs in the U.S. Through a nanoscale device, the movement of individual electrons was controlled. Single-electron devices depend on the tunnel effect. When two metallic electrons are separated by an insulating barrier about 1 nm thick, electrons begin tunneling through the insulator, which classical theory suggests is impossible. For digital electronics, researchers are trying to use SET transistors, but there is the problem of random variations in voltage from device to device. Researchers are trying to combat this problem. One day, traditional circuits will be replaced by electronics.

1988 (discovery of quantum dots):

An important contribution to nanotechnology was made by Dr. Louis Brus and his team in the early 1980s when they found that nano-sized crystal semiconductor materials made from the same substance exhibited strikingly different colors. These nanocrystal semiconductors were dubbed "quantum dots," and their research aided in the understanding of the quantum confinement effect, which explains the relationship and color of these nanocrystals. Due to their extraordinarily small size, the electrons inside the quantum dots exhibit unique behavior. Electrons, in particular, are restricted to far fewer energy levels than are permitted in bulk semiconductor materials.

This results in the quantum dots emitting very intense light of a specific color when the electrons make transitions between these discrete energy levels. Small differences in the size of the quantum dot have small differences in them that alter the energies of electrons and cause the color of the light to change. Scientists have learned how to control the size of quantum dots, making it possible to obtain a broad range of colors. Ways of improving medical diagnostics and collecting solar energy are revolutionized by quantum dots by providing efficient biological markers and advancing the development of optical devices such as light-emitting diodes (LEDs).

1990 (Manipulation of Atoms):

Researchers Donald Eigler and Erhard Schweizer arranged xe-atoms on a surface using STM. It was a painstakingly slow process to place individual xenon atoms with nanoscale precision and to visualize the results. This now-famous image of the atomic world "hangs" in IBM's STM Image Gallery and demonstrates early attempts to create structures one atom at a time.

1991 (Carbon nanotubes):

Sumi Iijima at NEC in Japan in 1991 developed a new form of carbon nanotubes that contained many tubes that nestled inside each other. Single-walled nanotubes about 1-2 nm in diameter were observed by Donald Bethune at IBM after two years. Electric current is conducted better by nanotubes than by copper, and nanotubes transmit heat better than diamonds and are very strong. They are between metals and semiconductors. In the practical uses of nanotechnology, nanotubes play a vital role.

1996 (Using DNA and Gold Colloids to Assemble Inorganic Materials):

Researchers have sought to exploit the optical properties of gold colloids since their discovery in 1857. In 1996, Northwestern University researchers Chad Markin and Robert Letsinger discovered a way to do this. They attached strands of synthetic DNA to gold nanoparticles. Since complementary strands of DNA can recognize and bind to each other, the DNA served as a blueprint, a construction worker, and a sorter to create new inorganic materials. By manipulating the DNA, they were able to make materials with the same unusual properties as the nanoscale building blocks that they are made from. This advance generated an explosion of interest in making designer bio-inorganic architectures at the nanoscale.

1999 (Development of Dip-Pen Nanotechnology):

A pivotal development in the constellation of nanotechnology tools was Dip-Pen Nanolithography, or DPN, invented in 1999 by Chad A. Mirkin. The concept is based on a classic quill pen, a 4,000-year-old technology. Chemicals, metals, biological macromolecules, and other molecules with links with nanometer dimensions can be laid down or written using DPN. Tiny, lighter-weight, faster, and more reliably created electronic circuits and devices, storage materials, and high-density biological and chemical sensors can be made from nano-manufacturing techniques, which are possible by including 1,000,000 tips of serial and parallel processing in DPN.

Pre-21st Century:-

2000 (feedback-controlled lithography):

Feedback-controlled lithography (FCL) is a technique that allows researchers to use the scanning tunneling microscope (STM) to precisely and selectively build structures at the nanoscale. Developed by Mark Hersam and Joseph Lyding, FCL is conducted by first coating a silicon sample with hydrogen (otherwise known as hydrogen-passivated silicon). The surface of the silicon sample can be seen using the STM. When electric voltage is applied to the STM tip from an outside source, the silicon-hydrogen bonds are broken. By controlling the position of the STM tip, hydrogen atoms are thus removed with atomic precision. This technique allows for fundamental studies of chemistry at the single-molecule level and has opened the door for building prototype devices and other structures at the nanoscale.

2002 (Laser-Assisted Direct Imprinting):

Laser Assisted Direct Imprinting (LADI) can increase transistor density in silicon chips 100-fold in only 10 to 20 minutes. It is completed by Chou's imprint method in a quarter of a millionth of a second.

2002 (Better than Silicon):

To help the nanotubes form, metals have been in great use for many years, but the problem is that they start containing the final product due to the soot formation, which must be filtered out. To construct the transistor arrays, various researchers developed a way for controlling the alignment of nanotubes. The nanotube transistor produced more than twice the current carrying capacity per unit width of top-performing silicon transistor prototypes, which have been outperformed by carbon nanotubes. A process was also developed for making the goal of using commercially available materials more attainable.

2002 (Nanoscale Soldering):

Nanowires can be created with a defect-less electrical junction by placing two different materials next to one another on the same nanometer-sized crystals. These types of nanowires in the form of building blocks have many uses in electronics, photonics, or biochemical detection.

2002 (Moving Toward a Molecular Future):

Researchers at Hewett-Packard [HPQ] and IBM began molecular electronics experiments by manipulating individual atoms and molecules to create logic gates and memory circuits. The chemical process used for creating molecular-scale electronic devices was unveiled by HP. It is also ordinary, cheap, and scalable. A technology called "molecular cascading" was created by IBM using this technique, and the world's smallest logic circuit was created.

2002 (super-dense hard drives):

Harsh Chopra's major discovery had serious implications for the magnetic storage industry. When electrons pass through metals, they scatter and bounce in different directions. Current is produced in a conductor, say a metal wire, when electrons flow and move in one direction. Chopra discovered that electron scattering ceases and electrons flow straight through a few nanometer-wide wires. For making chip components, a new method was demonstrated by IBM in 2003. The molecular self-assembly technique also avoids and minimizes the most severe tool transition and safety hazards. This technology depends on certain kinds of polymer molecules to arrange and organize themselves.

A pattern of polymer molecules is created using traditional methods such as lithography, and electronic devices such as microprocessors, which are used in a growing array of communication devices, computer chips, and consumer electronics, are created using self-assembly technologies. A high-speed 128 KB MRAM core was presented by IBM at the VLSI symposia in Kyoto, Japan. Because of the small size of the base, the two companies were able to incorporate MRAM memory cells measuring 1.4 square microns. Researchers controlled the memory's reading and writing operations by using magnetic structures within the small cell.

Magnetic field memory technology can store bits of data. By storing more information, accessing it faster, and using less battery power than electronic memory, MRAM can impoverish computing products. Storage capacity, low-cost DRAM, high-speed SRAM, non-volatility of flash memory, etc. are the characteristics or features of MRAM, today's common memory technique. Without waiting for software to boot up, if we turn off MRAM's power, then products like personal computers can be started in no time. A book named "Soft Machines" was written by Richard Jones in 2004 and published by Oxford University. It is about nanotechnology. In this book, radical nanotechnology is described as the mechanistic idea of nano-engineered machines. In these machines, challenges like wetness, stickiness, Brownian motion, etc. are not taken up. Biomimetic nanotechnology is also explained in this book, along with soft nanotechnology. Soft nanotechnology is thought to be the development of nanomachines from lessons taken from biology, which tells us how objects work, chemistry for the engineering of such devices, and its natural processes.

A new way was discovered in 2005 to make structures from RNA. Two-dimensional arrays and three-dimensional polygons were made from nucleic acids. Similarly, three-dimensional arrays can be made. Many times, researchers talk about the incorporation of these nanomachines into nanodevices. Within that time, a new direction was taken by the chemistry and molecular genetics communities. Simultaneously, synthesis was directed into either a modified living organism or a test tube. Many advances in controlling and manipulating light have been seen in the last quarter of a century. Light pulses can be shortened to a flow of femtoseconds. Light is measured on a 100-nanometer scale. Three strong techniques have met on the common nanoscale at the start of the new century. This will revolutionize both electronics and biology.

CHAPTER II

FUNDAMENTAL CONCEPTS AND APPROACHES OF NANOTECHNOLOGY

Introduction:-

Nanotechnology covers many fields or areas in life which are significant. It is the engineering of functional systems at the molecular scale. To produce full high-performance materials nanotechnology is used in many tools and devices. It is also used to construct items from the bottom up. One nm equals 10^{-9}. The scale range is 1-100 nm. According to the definition used by the National Nanotechnology Initiative in the United States (U. S). According to the size of atoms, a lower limit is set. Since nanotechnology makes its devices from atoms and molecules. 0.12-0.15 nm is the range of carbon-carbon bond lengths or the space present between the atoms. 2 nm is the diameter of D.N.A.

Molecular assembly operates molecular machines: that use individual atoms and molecules as working parts. Chemical bonds are made, broken, and rearrange by enzymes which work like molecular mechanisms at a rate of up to a million per second. DNA works as a digital storage medium. DNA direct ribosome's in manufacturing proteins in the human body. Nanotechnologies in the future will likewise be programmable molecular machines because it uses to build complex structure atom by atom.

Nanotechnology has two main approaches in the synthesis of nanomaterials and the fabrication of nanostructures.

Top-down approaches-

By use of lithography pattering, it constructs techniques nano-objects from a parent entity without atomic-level control. It refers to the slicing of bulk material to get nano-sized particles.

Bottom-up approaches-

The bottom-up approach builds the devices and material by the molecular component. The bottom-up approach makes the materials from atom by atom, molecule by molecule, and cluster by cluster.

Nanotechnology is an advanced technology. It can alter the way we live, and communicate on a mass scale. Never has any technology developed that has so much potential. The main concept of nanotechnology is the following create functional materials devices and systems by control of atoms and molecules on an atomic scale. Nanotechnology is first evolving in every sphere of life. It is the technology at a small scale when is submicron scale. Nanotechnology studies the properties of matter at a very small scale. On a nanometer scale, it has a broad ability to control the arrangements of atoms. This technology has different possibilities for the formation of structures like simple to complex structures, from larger to smaller dimensions, and molecular nanotechnology.

Romans and Chinese had no control over the particle size but they were using and manipulating nanoparticles thousands of years ago. The first nanotechnologists were Glass Walker. Based on nanotechnology manipulates the movement and stopping of particles it depending on how close together the molecules are and determines the ending color of the finished glass.

There are three branches of nanotechnology:-

1. Indirect branch

2. Direct branch

3. Conceptual branch

Indirect branch:

In this branch progressive miniaturization of existing technology opens up new areas of applications for these technologies. It is enabling technology. Miniaturizations can quantitatively perform and it becomes qualitative when a quantitative change is big enough a good example is the history ofthe cellular telephone.It is based on thermionic values; the circuitry for a cellular telephone would take up the volume of a long multistory building. The cell phone concept in 1950 became useful once because the circuits and their components become small enough to fit into a handset. All the applications of powerful computing are epiphenomena of nanotechnology.

Direct branch:

It refers to the applications of novel, nanoengineered artifacts, either to increase the performance of existing processes and materials or for wholly novel purposes. Nanoparticles and nanorobots are novel forms of matter are represent direct nanotechnology.For example, nano foil is made from thousands of alternative nanometer-size thick layers of two different metals, in short when an electrical pulse is applied across the foil to start mixing the two metals releases a large amount of heat. Any assemblage, small or large such as an airplane whose components are bounded together using this technique is a manifestation of nanotechnology.

Conceptual branch:

In this branch, all materials and processes are considered from a molecular or even atomic viewpoint, as in living systems, in which complicated molecules (proteins) are broken down into amino acids. Amino acids are then used for the synthesis of new proteins. In the conceptual nanotechnology survey, the structures are analyzed by considering the movement of each atom.

Approaches of nanotechnology:-

There are two approaches for the manufacturing of products namely Top-down and Bottom-up. The foresight institute, these approaches were first applied in the field of nanotechnology in 1989. Bottom-up approaches have small components so that they can be changed into more complex assemblies. On the other hand, top-down approaches have larger components and they make nanoscale devices using these components.

1. Bottom-up approaches:-

Prof. Feynman produced the atomic scale fabrication by using the bottom-up approach. Component, made of single molecules, will be provided by bottom-up manufacturing. Inductive reasoning is another name for a bottom-up approach. In many cases, it is used as a synonym for synthesis. This involves piecing together the systems and convert into a grand system. In the human body, information enters through the eyes and then goes into the human body in conserved parts, and input is turned into an image that can be interpreted and recognized like output.

The 'Seed' model is given for the understanding of the bottom-up approach. In the bottom-up approach, firstly individual base elements of the system are specified in great detail, and these elements then form larger subsystems. However "organic strategies" may result in a tangle of elements and subsystems. Object-orientated programming (OPP) is a paradigm. In mechanical engineering, OPP has many applications or uses along with software programmers. Materials or substances are firstly designed as pieces by auto desk invention and solid works and after this, these pieces are assembled to form buildings. We can call this piece part design mechanical engineering. One weakness is presented in the bottom-up approach. To decide by good intuition, the functionality that is to be provided by the module is essential. This system starts from existing modules. The engineer does never less hold.

Less wastage and strong covalent bonds will hold the constituent parts together with this technology. To form DNA by taking component molecules and then binding those together to produce the final structures all calls use enzymes. Other examples of bottom-up techniques include molecular fabricated ions, chemical synthesis, and self-assembly. Molecular fabrication is only one technique in these techniques where molecules or atoms are manipulated into position one by one. Consequently, it is a hardworking process that has addressed the problems of scaling up the technology to manufacture elements that are linked together and form larger subsystems.

These scenarios have been first proposed by the scientist Eric. Drexler has a suggestion of out of control replication leads to gray goo, experimental atomic and molecules, cosmetics, and some additives are instances of structures made using bottom-up techniques. We hope to produce small clusters of specific atoms to help replicate nature's ability. Atoms are produced by a chemical process that produces nanoparticles. The base of this technique is alternation in solution. For instance, chemical vapor deposition (CVD), sol-gel processing, and plasma or flame spraying synthesis.

- *The field of classical chemical synthesis (e.g. biopeptides) by the designing of molecules having well-defined shapes.*
- *In general, the concepts of supermolecular chemistry and molecular recognition are sought by molecular self-assembly so that single-molecule components can arrange themselves.*
- *The specific Watson Crick base pairing is used in DNA nanotechnology to produce well-defined structures of DNA and nucleic acids.*

Advantages of the bottom-up approach:-

- *The bottom-up approach has many uses in the area of business. It is used in business awareness of the product. It is in the early phases that its benefits are realized.*
- *With the help of this approach, we can substitute many manual processes with early automation.*
- *The implementation of password management can be accomplished with the help of a bottom-up approach.*
- *In the early phases, there is no need to develop custom adapters.*
- *During the first phase, understanding and identity management skills can be broadened.*

Disadvantages of the bottom-up approach:-

- *The bottom-up approach lacks democratic control and transparency. The actual power of policy-making is deferment as a result of faceless.*
- *From the individual-managed application, the direct implementation becomes a showcase.*

- *The first implementation becomes a showcase for the identity management solution.*
- *When the phases are completed for the managed application, a deeper, more mature implementation of the identity management solution takes place.*
- *The bottom-up approach can't influence the operation and maintenance resources.*

2. Top-down approaches:-

The Construction of parts through different ways such as cutting, molding, and curving can be achieved by a top-down approach. A remarkable variety of electronics and mechanical devices can be fabricated by these methods. Nevertheless, the sizes for making these devices are limited by our capability of curving, molding, and cutting. Top-down nanotechnology creates structures with limited dimensions by laying down thin layers of materials and by removing undesirable parts of the layers. Top-down nanotechnology is the natural extension of present ways of microelectronics.

Structures and mechanisms are miniature to the manometer scale from top to bottom particularly; this has proved to be the most frequent application of nanotechnology, especially in electronics where miniaturization is important. Material wastage is involved in this process and this process is limited by the resolution of tools, preventing the little sizes of structures created by these techniques. Many types of lithography techniques in this approach photo, ion beam, electron or x-rays-lithography cutting, etching, and grinding are involved. Lithography is a type of selection process which allows the patterning of the desired design onto the starting material.

On the other hand, the material left is exposed to ions, UV, X-rays, or electrons. After this, the surface is deposited leaving behind a desirable shape. After this, the surface is deposited leaving behind a desirable shape. To miniature electronic elements like computer chips, MEMS, DVD, CD players, etc. these techniques are utilized. Miniaturization of these materials is continued by Lithography. It is done to make Moore's law applicable.

A system is broken down to gain insight into compositional sub-systems. With the help of a top-down approach, it is also called stepwise design or deductive reasoning. With the help of block boxes, the specification of a top-down model is possible. This makes the manipulation easier. Nevertheless, it can be there that elementary mechanisms can't be elucidated by block boxes. The starting of the top-down approach takes place from the big picture. After that, it breaks down into little segments. Lithography is the most common top-down approach to fabrication. It includes the patterning of techniques using short-wavelength optical sources.

The top-down approach, produced in fabricated ions of integrated circuits, has the most important advantage in that parts are both built-in space and patterned so that no assembly space is required. Due to its high degree of refinement in the manufacturing of microelectronics chips, optical lithography is a mature field as short wavelength optical lithography techniques are reaching below 100nm dimensions. X-ray and ultraviolet which are short wavelengths sources are being developed to permit lithographic printing techniques to reach dimensions of 10nm-100nm. Electron beam lithography which is a scanning beam technology provides patterns of up to 20nm.

For patterning of wafers and direct processing, focused ion beams are utilized. For depositing and removing thin layers, still, tiny features are obtained by using scanning probes. Stamping, molding, and imprinting, which are mechanical printing techniques, have been extended to tiny dimensions of about 20-40nm. Stamps surface has a coating of a thin layer of products which is deposited on the surface and reproduces the stamp's surface. For instance, the patterning of a molecular monolayer can be controlled on a surface by achieving a stamp of ink thiol that functionalizes organic molecules directly onto a gold-coated surface.

The pattern can be presented into a thin layer of material by using the stamp in another approach. During the stamping procedure, the surface layer, which has been made pliable for the modeling process, is a polymeric material. Under stamped regions, plasma etching can be used to remove the thin layer of masking material. Any residual polymer can be removed by leaving a nanoscale lithographic pattern on the surface. Another variation is the formation of a relief pattern out of photo resists on a silicon wafer by optical or electron beam lithography and then pouring the liquid precursor like poly diethyl over the pattern and then curing it. A rubbery solid is formed as a result that can be peeled off and used as a stamp.

We can press these stamps on the surface and can make a liquid polymer to follow into raised regions of the mask by capillary action and treated in place. The stamp can be utilized to print nanoscale features on curved surfaces and also it is flexible. Particularly we can carry out these approaches in ordinary laboratories with less expensive equipment than used in conventional lithography. At the micro-scale, top-down technology can function well while at nanoscale dimensions it becomes difficult to apply them. This is the challenge of the top-down technique. The second disadvantage is that structures are formed by subtractions and the addition of patterned layers. This states that top-down technology includes the planner technique.

A complete and planned understanding of the system can be achieved by a top-down approach. On attaching the subs in place of modules, we can implement top-down approaches. Until the important design is completed, testing of the final functional units of the system is delayed. Early testing and coding are emphasized by a bottom-up approach which wills that soon. But the risk in this approach is that without having any idea how to link other parts of the system, modules can be coded, and also linking is not easy. One main benefit of the bottom-up approach is reusability.

Due to the engineering and management success of this project, the top-down approach is spread. Paper program development was written by Nicklaus Wirth by stepwise refinement. Wirth was also the developer of the Pascal programming language. He did not strictly promote top-down technology, since he went on the develop languages like Oberon and Modula. Top-down techniques were used in software engineering until the 1980s. OOP assisted both aspects of top-down and bottom-up programming. For directing their assembly smaller devices were created to use larger ones.

- *In this description, giant magnetoresistance hard drivers fit that are already on the market. For the invention of Giant magnetoresistance and contributions to the field of spintronics in 2007, Peter Gruenberg & Albert Fret were awarded Nobel prizes in Physics.*
- *Solid state technology can produce devices called nano-electromechanical systems or NEMS, which are concerned with micro-electromechanical systems or MEMS.*
- *When suitable precursor glasses are applied at the same time, focused ion beams can directly remove material. To produce sub-100nm sections of material for analysis in Transmission electron microscopy, this technology is used.*

Advantages of the top-down approach:-

- *Political and administrative responsibilities are represented by a top-down approach and they are clearly distinguished from each other by the relevant office holder, responsibility for political failure can be found.*
- *From the individual-managed application, focused use of resources can be realized.*

- *For the identity-managed solution, the first implementation becomes a showcase.*
- *A deeper and more mature implementation of the identity management solution takes place when the phases are finished for the managed applications.*
- *The bottom-up approach severely influences the operations and maintenance resources while this is not so in the case of a top-down approach.*

Disadvantages of the top-down approach:-

- *In the first phases, limited coverage is provided by the solution.*
- *In the first phase, a minimal % of user accounts is measured.*
- *Custom adapters might need to develop at an early stage.*
- *The cost of implementation of this approach is very high.*
- *The benefit of the solution will not be realized or supported very fastly.*
- *Inferiors are demotivated by this system as they know that their decisions will not be accepted by the decision-makers and also their approaches will not be welcomed.*

Top-down approach v/s Bottom-up approach:-

An important top-down approach includes a system for gaining insight into its compositional sub-system is first formulated but the first-level subsystems are not detailed. After that, until the whole specification is decreased to base elements, each subsystem including additional subsystem levels is refined in greater detail. In other words, the meaning of the top-down approach is to decompose the solution procedure into subtasks. Molecular and readable code is produced by this approach that can be maintained and understood easily. The bottom-up approach makes the subsystems of the original system the emergent system.

Differentiate the Top-down and Bottom-up approaches with an example:-

Let us imagine a tree-like structure. If we apply a bottom-up approach to this structure then we will move from the leaf node. On the other hand, if we apply a top-down approach to this structure then we will from the root node to the leaf node.

- *Bottom-up design proceeds from concrete design for obtaining the abstract entity while the abstract entity is preceded by top-down design to obtain the concrete design.*

- *Bottom-up and top-down designs are both combined in real life off and on. For example, bouncing back and forth between top-down and bottom-up modes, data modeling sessions tend to be iterative.*
- *In designing brand-new systems, top-down design is used. On the other hand, bottom-up design is used when one is trying the figure out what somebody else designed. In other words, bottom-up design is used in the reverse engineering of a design.*
- *An overview of the system is first formulated in the top-down approach but first-level subsystems are not detailed while individual base elements are first specified in great detail in the bottom-up approach.*
- *Top-down designs start the design with the top-level or main module and then progress down words to the subsystems or lowest-level modules and then progress up words to the top-level or main module. Bottom-up design on the other hand starts the design with a subsystem or lowest-level modules and then progresses up words to the top-level or main module.*

Functional approaches:-

Components of the desired functionality are developed by these approaches. Molecular, having useful electronics properties can be developed by molecular scale electronics. In nano-electronic devices, these can be used as single-molecule components.

Biomimetic approaches:-

- *In bionanotechnology, biomolecules are used for applications in nanotechnology along with the use of viruses.*
- *Natural biological methods and systems are applied to the design and study of modern technology and engineering systems in bio-memory or bionics. One instance of the system studied is biomineralization.*

Other approaches:-

What discoveries nanotechnology can yield, can be anticipated by these subfields. These approaches can take a lot of view of nanotechnology along with its emphasis on societal implications.

- *Manipulating single molecules, in deterministic and controlled ways is included in molecular nanotechnology.*

- *Nanorobotics can be used on machined which are self-sufficient. Nanorobotics might be applied in medicine but due to several limitations and drawbacks of such kind of devices, it is not easy. However with some patents granted for new manufacturing devices, progress on innovative methods and illustrated. Development towards nanorobots is also assisted by these devices along with the use of nano bioelectronics methods.*
- *Productive nanosystems are usually systems of nanosystems and they create precise parts for either nano-system. It is not necessary to produce these parts using novel nanoscale emergent properties. Four stages of nanotechnology, then seen the parallel to the technical progress of the Industrial Revolution, is one of the architects of USA's Nationals Nanotechnology Initiative, Michael Rocco. These four states of nanotechnology complex nanomachines and at the end program to productive nanosystems.*
- *The terms Femto technology and biotechnology have been coined in analogy due to the media exposure and popularity of the term nanotechnology.*
- *Programmable matter can design materials having properties that can be easily, reversibly, and externally controlled.*

Larger to samaller: a material perspective:-

As the size of the system reduces the number of physical phenomena becomes pronounced. These phenomena involve quantum mechanical effect which is included in statically mechanical impacts. By going from macro to micro dimensions, quantum size effects can't come into play. For instance increment in surface area to volume ratio. This change affects the mechanical, optical, and electrical properties. Nanoionics are generally referred to the nanostructures or nanodevices with rapid ion transport. Potential risks are opened by the catalytic activity of nanomaterials in their interaction with biomaterials. As compared with the properties exhibited by the materials at the macro scale, the properties at the nanoscale are different. For example, stable materials become combustible; opaque substances become transparent; insoluble substances become soluble. Even if gold is chemically non-reactive, it can become a potent chemical catalyst at the nanoscale.

Simple to complex: a molecular perspective:-

The point where little molecules can be prepared for any structure has been reached by modern synthetic chemistry. Along with the seeking methods to ensemble these single molecules into supermolecular ensembles lies, for manufacturing a lot of useful chemicals like pharmaceuticals or commercial polymers, these methodologies are being used today. By a bottom-up approach, to arrange them into some useful conformation, these approaches use the concepts of molecular self-assembly or surface molecular chemistry. Molecules may be designed to favor a specific arrangement or configuration due to the noncovalent intermolecular forces.

Devices should be prepared by bottom-up approaches that are parallel and also cheaper than top-down approaches but these should be overwhelmed as the complexity and the size desired assembly enhances. Complex and thermodynamic arrangements of atoms are noted as the most useful structures. However, including the Watson- crick base pairing and enzyme-substrate interactions, there are a lot of instances of self-assembly in biology based on molecular recognition. Whether the principles can be used in addition to natural ones, is the challenge for nanotechnology.

Molecular nanotechnology: a long - term view:-

Engineered nanosystems operating on the molecular scale are described in molecular nanotechnology also known as molecular manufacturing. Molecular assembler is concerned with molecular nanotechnology and can make the desired structure. Traditional techniques were used to manufacture nanomaterials like nanoparticles and carbon nanotubes. Manufacturing is a productive nanosystem. It is associated with industrial activities.

The term nanotechnology was coined and popularized by Eric Drexler. Drexler and other researchers proposed that advanced nanotechnology may be based on the mechanical functionality of components such as bearing motor gear etc. Nanotechnology can make impressive progress in many spheres by using biomimetic principles. This would enable the positional and programmable assembly to atomic specification. Generally assembling devices on an atomic scale is not easy since atoms gas to be positioned on other atoms of comparable stickiness and size. The view that future nanosystems will form a base of hybrids of silicon technology and biology molecular machines was put forward or given by Carla Monte Mango. Again according to Richard Smalley, mechanic synthesis is possible because of the difficulties in mechanically manipulating individual molecules.

In the ACS publication chemical and engineering News, an exchange of letters took place in 2003, and it is demonstrated by biology that molecular machine systems possible at Lawrence Berkeley are the leaders in research on nonbiological molecular devices, whose motion is controlled from the desktop with changing potential difference. A molecular actuator and a nanoelectromechanical relaxation oscillator have been constructed by particles such as nanotubes and nanomotor. Lee experimented in 1999 at Cornell University for indicating that positional molecular assembly is possible. Scanning tunneling microscope has been proposed that shortly environmentally clean efficient and cheap manufacturing of old devices, smart products, and structures may be feasible which are based upon the flexible control of processes and architecture at molecular or an atomic scale. Complex products can be created by using raw materials such as inserting the basic chemical elements in a molecular assembly factory. This is to yield a common household appliance. Impressive demonstrations have been made by using microscope devices. For instance, the smallest micromechanical 0.3 um wide was made by scientists from Osaka University in august 2001. One cannot imagine a scenario in which quantum switch-based computing molecular computers or else could offer an important performance benefit at a competitive price, provided that the virtual certainty of continued progress is given in this area.

CHAPTER III

NANOPARTICLES

Introduction:-

Any small object can be defined as a particle in nanotechnology if it behaves or functions as a whole unit concerning its properties and transport. Further classifications of particles are based according to the diameter. Nanoparticles are the ones that have many dimensions and have the order of 100 nm or less. There are still many discussions going on about the size of nanoparticles. Some believe the size there must be below 100 nm. On the one hand, their size is said to be less than 100 nm. It is said that they must have a size of less than 100 nm. Nanoparticles of size less than 100 nm are called first-generation nanoparticles while nanoparticles of size less than 1000 nm are called ad second-generation's nanoparticles. Approximately 1 nm is considered as the lower limit for the size of nanoparticles.

The size of nanoparticles that are coarse is between 2500 to 100 nm. Nanoparticles are also called ultrafine particles which have a size range between 1 to 100 nm. Some object has been given two different names. Its cause or reason is that when nanoparticles were being studied first in the United States of America by Granqvist and Buhrmann and Japan with the ERATO project their name was ultrafine particles (UFP). This happened during the 1970s-1980s. The word nanoparticles come into use during the 1990s before the launching of the National Nanotechnology Initiative in the U. S. A. The characteristics of fine particles or bulk materials are different fine particles. We can't refer to individual molecules as nano-particles.

The general term 'nanoparticles' is sometimes used for covering the materials which are better explained or described using another term. A no. of transistors in physical properties can occur when macro particles changes to nanoparticles.

The dominance of the behavior of atoms that are at the surface of particles enhances when the surface area to volume ratio increases and particles get smaller. These atoms are present in the interior of the particles. Due to this, the properties of the particle are affected both in isolation as well as in interaction with other materials. The strength, chemical, or heat resistance of intermixed materials is increased by the large surface area of nanomaterials in nanocomposites. A large surface area is also important for the performance of catalysis. It is very slow to change classical mechanics to quantum mechanical behavior once they become small enough to do so. When free electrons in an atom start to behave like those bound by atoms then they are called artificial atoms. Nanoparticles are very useful in packaging, cosmetics, and coatings due to their property of transparency which is rendered to them when they have dimensions below the wavelengths of light. If we try to understand only the influence of nanoparticles on surface atoms then we can't simply predict their properties. For instance; it has been shown that if silicon nanospheres are formed with a diameter of between 10 to 100 nm then they not only become harder but they will be among the hardest known materials between Diamond and sapphire. The most famous examples of nanoparticles are carbon black. Almost 1.5 million tonnes of materials are created every year.

Nanotechnology can be applied to the Carbon black industry to the new production and analysis at the nanoscale and advances in theoretical understanding. The ceramics can be easily split into metal oxide ceramics like titanium, Zinc, aluminum, and iron oxides. Thus nanoparticles are made out of these types of materials. There are many definitions of nanoparticles but accepted definitions. This size is less than 100 nm but many new applications use the size range of about 100 nm. The size of nanoparticles used in metals and metal oxide ceramics nanopowders is from two or three up to a few hundred nanometers.

The nanoparticles of pure metal can undergo the process of sintering which is the process of merging nanoparticles into a solid, without meeting at a lower temperature. This will help to create coatings in electronic applications like capacitors. Metal oxide ceramics nanoparticles are useful in creating crystalline or amorphous layers.

At lower temperatures, we can form ceramic nanoparticles into coating and bulk materials. It will also reduce the cost of manufacturing. Conventional ceramics materials were brittle while those made from ceramic nanoparticles are flexible. U. S. Navy uses nanocrystalline ceramics for its research work. In 2001, the process of forming a substance called Chitosan from nanoparticles was completed. We use these substances in our hair conditioners and skin creams which improve absorption. A lot of nanoparticles having present and hopeful uses are constituted in metal silicate nanoparticles. The applications in various fields increase the importance of nanotechnology. The biological and medical research communities have explained the unique properties of nanoparticles

History of nanoparticles:-

Their history is older even than nanotechnology. Nanoparticles were first used in the 9th century in Mesopotamia. The objective behind their use was the creation of a shiny and attractive effect on the surfaces of posts. Due to gold and copper colored metallic's, pots had a shiny appearance from the middle ages and Renaissance period. This shining could be created by making a metallic film and then applying it to a transparent surface of covering. The glitter was visible until the oxidation and weathering conditions continued on the film silver and copper nanoparticles were present in the glitter. After the object was created, it was heated in a special oven up to 600°C in reducing atmosphere. On adding salts of copper and silver and then oxides them with clay, vinegar, etc. on the surface nanoparticles were produced by artisans.

Nanoparticles were formed when the ions come together and then they gave their effects and color. Even today, gold and copper-colored glitter are retained in pottery. It is due to the application of metallic film on the transparent surface of glazing until the film resists oxidation and weathering, the luster can be visible or seen. Luster originated in the film having copper and silver nanoparticles. On the surface of previously glazed pottery, many substances like copper and silver salts, oxides vinegar, clay, ochre, etc. were added.

Artisans added their materials to create nanoparticles. First of all, the object is placed in the kiln and heated at about 600° C in the decreasing atmosphere. Due to rising temperature, the glaze would become soft and to the surface of the glaze, silver and copper ions would come. As a result of decreasing atmosphere, ions will come together forming nanoparticles. The Luster technique originated in the Islamic world. Muslims were prevented from using gold in their artistic representations. Hence they discovered a solution to create this impact without using real gold. The use of luster was the solution. Wise experiments and knowledge of ancient craftsmen have been proven and shown by the Glitter method.

The glitter method originated in the Islamic world where Muslim people had no right to use glad in their artistic representation. Hence they attended to create a similar look for their tasks and they found the glitter method. This glitter method proved that the ancient craftsmen had wise experimental knowledge about these materials. The origin of this technique is Islamic art as Muslim people were forbidden to use gold in artistic work, therefore they originated this technique and attempted to produce a similar look to gold for their works and the solution was the glitter method. This is also used on a Roman cup, which is called a Lycurgus cup.

This cup had gold clusters on it to create different colors on it. It has been also discussed from different sources that, the first usage of nanoparticles was found in early dynasty Chinese porcelain. In his 1857 paper, Michael Faraday stated the characteristics and properties of nanometer-scale metals. Turner, the author of the subsequent paper, stated that when we place thin gold and silver leaves on a glass and heat them to a temperature less than red heat then the transition of properties takes place. The metallic film gets ruined. Its consequences include the diminishing of white light and increasing electrical resistivity.

Various types of nanoparticles:-

Nanoparticles have adverse effects on medicine and the environment. Particles are made highly reactive by the high surface-to-volume ratio. Particles can go inside the body of living organisms by passing through the plasma membranes and interacting with their biological systems.For labeling certain molecules, structures, or microorganisms, magnetic nanoparticles bound to a suitable antibody are used. For detecting genetic sequence in the sample, gold nanoparticles tagged with short segments of DNA can be used.

By depositing the active agent in the morbid region, the overall drug consumption and side effects can be reduced. Gold nanoparticles are considered letter for targeted drug delivery than cheaper types of nanoparticles like iron nanoparticles. Gold nanoparticles are attached to a diseased region of the body by researchers. These regions may be cancer tumors of therapeutic drug molecules. This thing makes the gold nanoparticles able to provide some contribution to targeted drug delivery. This has been shown by a recent study. Regulatory approval is sought by many pharmaceutical companies. Pre-reformulation versions could result in regulatory bodies such as FDA, following aside new side effects that are specific or unique to nano-reformulation. The health hazards caused by nanoparticles present in cosmetics and sunscreens are still unknown. Nevertheless, it has been demonstrated that damage to the cardiovascular system in a mouse model is caused by diesel nanoparticles. It is also found that Zinc nanoparticles are not absorbed in the bloodstream. The protection of nanoparticles has been examined by the environment protection agency and this examination is underway as of 2013.

Iron nanoparticles:-

Iron an element in its bulk form has many uses in everyday life. It is used to stain railways and structural beams in cars and buildings. Iron helps transport oxygen in the water and our blood. Iron is used for making magnets. Rusting of iron takes place due to its aerial oxidation whose product is iron oxide. It is a fact that all electrons spin. On aligning the spin of unpaired electrons to a magnetic field, we can form a magnet. Each atom of iron contains four unpaired electrons which state that they can be aligned to change any piece of iron into a magnet. Magnetic properties of iron are also retained in the nanoparticles that have increased surface area like iron oxide.

It makes the iron nanoparticles helpful in medical imaging and cleaning effluents in groundwater. Iron nanoparticles are useful in medical imaging and treatments as follows:-

- *Targeted drug delivery: Drugs can be delivered into a patient's body at a particular place by using iron nanoparticles.*
- *Improved MRI imaging and treatment: when nanoparticles are concentrated in a diseased region then diseased cells can be killed by using a magnetic electric field.*

Iron nanoparticles clean the groundwater pollutants by giving electrons to more electronegative atoms like chlorine atoms. This donation of electrons is useful for breaking harmful molecules into harmless molecules. Iron nanoparticles are used to treat large areas of groundwater because they can be suspended for a long time in groundwater and then transported to the whole system.

Iron oxide nanoparticles:-

Iron oxide is formed due to the oxidation of iron with oxygen. Also when the iron is left in rain, it starts resulting and rust is an iron oxide that contains three atoms of iron and four atoms of oxygen. Iron oxide also has magnetic properties. Iron oxide has only two unpaired electrons as compared to iron. As we know that unpaired electrons make a material magnetic, and iron is more magnetic than iron oxide. Another name for iron oxide is paramagnetic material.

The paramagnetic properties of iron oxide nanoparticles are not altered from bulk material. The only thing is that these small particles can go where large particles never could. A better image is formed when an object is taken and attached to paramagnetic magnetic resonance imaging nanoparticles. It is the reason that researchers are using iron oxide nanoparticles for getting better images in MRI. Researchers have made these nanoparticles which have iron oxide nanocrystals encircled by nanoporous silica so that MRI images can be improved and they could control the release of therapeutic drugs.

Arsenic, a natural substance found in soil, is a major problem for people throughout the world as it can dissolve in water including water from wells.

Robert Bunsen, who discovered Bunsen burner which can be seen in high school science labs, demonstrated that if the iron oxide is mixed with arsenic thin fluids in our body as well as in water can't be broken down. Due to his discovery, iron oxide is used in filters to remove arsenic from water.

Gold nanoparticles:-

Gold element is used in coins, jewelry, electronic devices, dentistry, etc. even we use gold in some medicines. Bulk gold is an unreactive or inert material that does not tarnish or corrode. Similar to all metals, gold has good thermal and electrical conductivity. It is used in electronic devices because of its resistivity and high electrical conductivity. With harmless effects, gold is being used in various kinds of medical treatments for many years. Hence it was obvious that researchers appreciated gold nanoparticles for medicine rather than elements like platinum which may prove to be toxic and harmful. Bulk gold could not reach some areas that are too small so gold was changed into nanoparticles for efficiency. Gold nanoparticles are considered letter for targeted drug delivery than cheaper types of nanoparticles like iron nanoparticles. Gold nanoparticles can be used as a catalyst when they become small even less than the diameter of 5 nm. At that stage, they can even change air pollutants into harmless molecules.

It is not wise to talk to use gold as a catalyst for chemical reactions because it can't help too much in that field. If gold is broken to a nanosize then it can oxidize carbon monoxide by behaving as a catalyst. Gold nanoparticles are attached to a diseased region of the body by researchers. These regions may be cancer tumors of therapeutic drug molecules. This thing makes the gold nanoparticles able to provide some contribution to targeted drug delivery. Gold nanoparticles can change wavelengths of light into heat gold has free electrons which can move throughout the metal. The electrons are not tied to a particular atom. The movement of these electrons makes the electric current pass through a conductor when potential differences are applied to it. It has been found that the following two kinds of gold nanoparticles shapes are more feasible and efficient in converting light into heat:

Gold nanorods:-

They are cylindrical and have a diameter of around 10 nm. Scientists can alter the wavelength of light absorbed by nanorods by using them, with different combinations of diameter and length.

Nanospheres:-

They are made of a gold coating over a silica core. With variations in the thickness of the gold coating and the diameter of the silica core, researchers can change the wavelength of light absorbed by nanospheres. Researchers are either using nanospheres of roads for "yperthermia therapy". In this method heat treatment is applied to the diseased regions of the body for getting relief.

Platinum nanoparticles:-

Platinum is found very rarely. As it is both in jewelry and as a catalyst, its demand is throughout the world. But in the form of a catalyst, it is very costly and also very effective. Possibly, we use platinum in the catalytic converter as a catalyst daily. Air-polluting particles from car exhaust are transformed into less harmful particles by the platinum in the catalytic converter. When the bonding of platinum atoms takes place with atoms in the molecular like hydrogen, hydrogen atoms are released by platinum atoms and then hydrogen atoms react `with other molecules.

The chemical reactions are facilitated by platinum atoms on breaking up molecules into atoms. The surface area available for a reaction is enhanced by the platinum nanoparticles and also the % of platinum atoms available for contact with other molecules in a reaction is enhanced. It is due to this difference that researchers and scientists use small quantities of platinum. Air pollutants can be broken down and the cost of catalysts used in fuel cells is decreased by these improved catalysts. Nanotechnologists can lay other options in some cases looking at the high value of platinum. The material used to make glass is silicon dioxide on silica.

Naturally, the quartz sand on the beach is made of silica. Silica has poor thermal and electrical conductivity. Silica aerogels are made of silica nanoparticles interspersed with nanoporous filled mostly, this material is made up of air as a result. Both silica and air are good substances to be used as insulators because of their property of conducting very low heat. Nanoaerogels can be made beat thermal insulators due to these properties. On bonding molecules to nanoparticles, silica nanoparticles can be functionalized. Water repellency effect can be given to lotus leaves by attaching functionalized silica nanoparticles to a cotton fiber and creating a rough hydrophobic surface. With nanoscale pores, another kind of silica nanoparticle is riddled. A drug delivery method is being developed by researchers where therapeutic molecules, stored in the pores, are released slowly in a diseased area of the body like that of a cancer tumor. For providing electrical insulation between two parts of a device like a transistor, silicon dioxide nanofilms of about 1 nm are used. Computer chips are made by using this method.

Silver nanoparticles:-

Like gold, silver is also used in Jewellery, coins, dentistry, and electronic devices. Silver has also been used in killing bacteria. When antibiotics were not discovered, silver was used to prevent infection in wounds. Silver has good thermal and electrical conductivity. Silver nanoparticles have a large no. of atoms at the surface. Silver nanoparticles have more ions at the surface and for this reason, they are used as an antimicrobial agent in the following ways:-

- *Silver nanoparticles are used in form of crystalline for the treatment of wounds.*
- *They are also used in plastic food storage bins so that if any bacteria are there in previously stored food then they can be killed.*
- *The microbes which can't live around silver ions produce small which are destroyed by silver nanoparticles.*
- *Silver nanoparticles are used to make a low-cost filter from silver nanowires and carbon nanotubes so that bacteria present in drinking water can be killed.*

Titanium dioxide nanoparticles:-

Titanium dioxide can use energy in light to catalyze reactions with other molecules at lowered temperatures i.e. Titanium dioxide nanoparticles are photocatalysts. Titanium dioxide performs best in sunlight so it is mostly used by researchers even if other photo-catalytic materials are available in the market. Light reflected by titanium dioxide is white as it reflects all colors of visible light. This property makes it useful as a white pigment in paints and it also makes for the white that resides on our skin when we lather on sunscreen. More effective nanoparticles can be formed by titanium dioxide nanoparticles as they have more surface area to react with other molecules. Titanium dioxide can be used in creams and coatings in its nanoparticle form which will absorb UV rays without causing a white coating. Titanium dioxide which contains one atom of titanium and two atoms of oxygen nanotubes is in hollow cylinders similar to carbon nanotubes. Titanium dioxide nanotubes contain molecules of titanium dioxide bonded together to form a cylindrical surface. After bonding to other titanium atoms, oxygen atoms starts with a cylindrical lattice in which two titanium atoms are bonded with each oxygen atom. This arrangement of oxygen and titanium atoms provides a complex structure of the nanotube.

A team of researchers led by Craig Grimes at Penn State has discovered a way of changing CO_2 into methane (CH_4). For this purpose, titanium dioxide tubes were used which were coated with a catalyst that changes CO_2 and H_2O

into CH_4 using sunlight energy as a source for carrying out chemical reactions. Cancer tumors can be destroyed by using the photo-catalytic properties of titanium dioxide nanoparticles. Titanium dioxide nanoparticles are delivered to cancer tumors by using a targeted drug delivery method and after that light is shown on the tumor. Titanium dioxide nanoparticles add electrons to oxygen molecules by using the energy from this light. This process or system can destroy or ruin cancer cells and makes the cancerous tumor.

Structure and properties of nanoparticles:-

Nanoparticles are like a connection point between atomic structures and bulk materials which is their most important property in science. Therefore, the properties of nanoparticles cannot be assumed as the same with bulk materials. Between bulk substances and atomic structures, nanoparticles are considered like a bridge. On the other hand percentage of atoms is not significant at the surface of bulk materials that are larger than one micrometer. The properties of materials can be interesting as well as unexpected because of their large surface area. Nanoparticles are very small in size to confine the electrons and create quantum effects. The melting point of gold nanoparticles is about 300^0 C, which is very low. On the other hand, 1064 ^{0}C is the melting point of gold slap. Materials composed of nanoparticles have a high absorption of solar radiation in photovoltaic cells.

It will make those materials unsuitable for memory storage. At high temperatures, nanoparticles provide a high driving force for diffusion because of the high surface area-to-volume ratio. Sintering takes place over shorter time scales at lower temperatures. Even the tendency of nanoparticles to agglomerate complicates matters of the density of final products and is not influenced by this theory. Many properties of nanoparticles are concerned with day-to-day products, for instance, the self-cleaning effect is due to the presence of titanium dioxide. Superior UV-blocking properties are found in the zinc oxide particles. That's why Zinc oxide particles are completely photo-stable and are used in preparing sunscreen lotions. Nanotechnology has the major advantage of making things very smaller. Nanotechnology is based on nanoparticles and their wonderful properties. It has resolved around the study of nanoparticles that they are very useful in every field of life. This is due to their property of behaving as a bridge between bulk materials and atomic or molecular structures.

We can conclude that as the size of particles reaches the nanoscale, the properties of materials experience great change. It has been seen that nanoparticles have a big importance in people's lives, especially in these last years. Studies show that it has been expected a huge future for the usage of nanoparticles in multi areas. However, it has been considered the economic, social, and environmental face of nanoparticles, which is not can be ignored. As compared to gold slabs, gold nanoparticles melt at a much lower temperature. The materials composed of nanoparticles absorb the solar radiations of photovoltaic cells much higher than thin films of continuous sheets of materials. Solar absorption will be increased as the size of particles is decreased. It means that solar absorption is adversely proportional to the particle's size.

The transitions in the physical properties are not desirable all the time. Their magnetization direction is switched by ferromagnetism below 10nm size. Surface Plasmon resonance and superparamagnetism in magnetic materials are involved in size-dependent property changes.Three nanoparticles give their properties to the polymer and are very strong. Nanoparticles are attached to textile fibers for producing smart clothing. Along with hybrid structures, dielectric and semiconductor nanoparticles have been created. Nanoparticles made of semi-conducting material may have quantum dots labeled on them. In biomedical such nanoscale particles are used as drug carriers or imaging agents. Liposomes are the one kind of nanoparticle that has semi-solid nature.There are many kinds of liposome nanoparticles are have at present uses in medicine as carriers of anticancer drugs and vaccines. At water/oil interfaces they can self-assemble and act as solid surfactants.

It should be seen that nanoparticles have such a wide variety if they are wanted to be defined in a category. Their structure and properties show differences between each of their components of them. Some examples of this situation can be seen below:-

Fullerenes: buckyballs and carbon tubes:-

They are like lattices and are highly porous molecules. They are carbon-based. Carbon tubes have cylindrical shapes while the shape of Buckyballs is spherical. The diameter of carbon tubes can be enhanced up to served mm, but the actual size is just several nm. Due to their strength and unique electrical properties, carbon nanotubes are used in material science. They are used in drugs and vaccines as carriers. It is any molecule made wholly of carbon. It can be a hollow sphere, ellipsoid tube, and many other forms. Buckyballs resemble the balls used in footballs and they are spherical fullerenes. On the other hand, cylindrical fullerenes are called buck tubes or carbon non-tubes. Buckminster Fuller was named after Buckminster Fuller a famous American Architect. This happened because the structure of Buckminsterfullerene resembled the framework of dome-shaped halls designed by Fuller for large American exhibitions.

Liposome:-

Liposomes are lipid-based nanoparticles. They can break down inside the cells, that's the reason that they are being used in cosmetic and pharmaceutical industries, for drug delivery they are engineered and used first but when they are faced with water, they show a propensity to face together, so instead of liposome's, scientists are using never alternative nanoparticles.

Nanoshells:-

They have a spherical shape and are made of spherical compounds. They have just a few nm thick shells or coatings around them. They are used in biomedicine for their good absorption of biologically useful wavelengths, depending on the shell thickness.

Dendrimers:-

They have natural hooks on their surfaces. Cell- identifications tags, fluorescent dyes, enzymes, and other molecules can be attached to them by using these hooks. They have been used for biotechnological uses recently since their production way in the year 1980.

Quantum dots:-

These are dependent upon their size changes and also these are semi-conductors. They can spread light in every color in the white light. Quantum dots lock up the band electrons, valance band gaps, or exactions in all three spatial directions. The most popular examples of quantum dots are Semiconductor nanocrystals and core shells nanocrystals. They have many uses in biotechnology like cell labeling, imaging, etc.

Superparamagnetic nanoparticles:-

They have their attachment to the magnetic field but the remaining magnetism is not saved by them once the field is removed. Iron oxide which is one of the nanoparticles in this group is used in bioseparation as a selective magnet. This iron oxide has a diameter range between 5-100 nm. They are especially being used as a coating in biological tissues.

Nanorods:-

Made from semiconducting materials nanorods have a size of 1-100 nm. They are used as imaging and contrasting agents in nanomedicine by generating tiny cylinders of silicon, gold, or inorganic phosphate. Low dimensions, which are below the wavelengths of light, are the important characteristics of nanoparticles. So they became really useful for packaging, cosmetics, and coatings application. Usually, nanoparticles are in two or three dimensions, in additions by a well-known natural process which is called crystallization nanoparticles can be upgraded to three-dimensional organizations of atoms, ions, or molecules. The similar particles which have different dimensions (one is two the other is three) show different properties. This also proves the size difference creates a big difference in the properties of the same nanomaterials. On the contrary, nanoparticles can be hard; for example, being produced superconducting wires by using ceramic nanoparticles despite the brittle property of ceramic bulk material. At very high temperatures they have a great driving force for diffusion, due to the surface area to volume ratio for nanoparticles.

With a raise in this ratio as the particle gets smaller, the surface atoms start to be more dominant in their behaviors than the ones interior which situations cause a decrease in the incipient melting temperature of the nanoparticles. The critical factor is created in the catalysis due to the high ratio. This also has its uses in batteries and fuel cells. Due to the increased ratio, nanoparticles become stronger and have high resistance to heat and chemicals.

Preparation of nanoparticles:-

Many technologies are involved in the preparation of nanoparticles. In the field of material science and ceramic engineering, the sol-gel process is widely used. For fabrications of materials, we can use such methods. This can be initiated with a chemical solution which is like a precursor for an integrated network of discrete particles. Metal oxides and metal chlorides are typical precursors, and they undergo hydrolysis and polycondensation reactions. A system of discrete sub-micrometer particles sub-micrometer particles dispersed to various degrees in most fluids is called colloidal suspension. Metal oxide can be produced by connecting metal centers with oxide or hydroxide bridges. Metal oxo or metal hydro-oxo polymer are generated in the solution as a result.

A gel-like biphasic system is formed which has both solid and liquid phases. The easiest and most common method is giving the sedimentation process some time to occur and then filtering the remaining liquid. For increasing the phase of separation, the centrifugation process can also be used. We require a drying process for removing the remaining liquid. This process also involves densification and shrinkage. The porosity distribution of the gel decides the rate at which the solvent is to be removed. Changes during the processing phase influence or affects the microstructure of the final component to increase the mechanical properties and structural ability of materials. Thermal treatment also called the firing process is necessary. Densification is done or achieved at a very low temperature. It is the distinct temperature of using this method. We can synthesize powders by using precursor solutions which can be other either deposited or substrates to form a film.

We can control the chemical composition of products by using the sol-gel approach which is an inexpensive and low-temperature technology. We can also introduce small dopants in the sol such as organic soil. We can also use this technique as an investment casting material used in manufacturing. It has also been used in the ceramic industry. Materials obtained from sol-gel have diverse uses in optics, electronics, energy, space, and separation technology. If tetraethyl orthosilicate(TEQS) undergoes hydrolysis under acidic conditions then SiO_2 *is formed in the form of monoliths and fibers. Due to this sol-gel technique becomes important.*

Usages of nanoparticles:-

Nanoparticles are used in many fields of science depending on their properties. They are used in medical applications, cosmetics, packaging, water paper treatment, pharmacy, etc. Also for manufacturing ferrofluids, magnetic recording media, drugs, cosmetics, phosphors, rocket propellant fuel additives, filler points, etc. Nanoparticles are being used in army defense applications as Fuel additives.

Usage in water treatment and purification:-

In the water purification area, nanoparticles are used because of their efficient removal of germs and pollutants from wastewater. Their working scale is a nanoscale, so they are good at cleaning waste. Therefore nanoparticles, nanopowder, and nanomembranes are used to detect and remove chemical biological substances including nutrients, metals, cyanide, organics, viruses, bacteria, parasites, and antibiotics.

Nanoparticles are compared to other treatment methods, like one of the most efficient ones. Chlorine and Bromine halogens are good at keeping the water away from bacteria, but the direct usage of these halogens as bactericides may create dangerous problems, because of their light toxicity and vapor pressure in pure form. By the high surface area to volume ratio, good better results are produced. In the coming time, it is suggested that we should use this ratio efficiently in large amounts of water.

Usage in medicine and biology:-

In medicine and biology, nanoparticles are one of the basic things for application. The most common and known uses of nanoparticles are the following-

- *They are useful in fluorescent biological labels.*
- *They are also used in the delivery of gens and drugs.*
- *They are used to detect pathogens.*

- *They are used to probe DNA structures.*
- *They are considered good for tissue engineering.*
- *They have also proved successful in destroying tumors by heating.*
- *With the help of nanoparticles biological cells and molecules and purified.*
- *They are used in toothpaste.*
- *They are used in phase kinetic studies.*
- *They are used in MRI contrast enhancement.*

Nanoparticles are used for biological processes such as labeling and tagging because they have the same size. As proteins have. For interacting with biological targets, nanoparticles, nanoparticles should be attached to bioinorganic interfaces which act as a biological or molecular layer or coating. For instance, biopolymers like collagen or monolayer of small molecules make nanoparticles biocompatible. The optical properties of nanoparticles can be altered for optical detection. They are used to recover damages and make hip or new prostheses in tissue engineering. However, especially in medical and biology applications, while studying nanoparticles, their toxicity factor should not be forgotten.

So this situation creates a high toxicity factor, showing different effects on human beings and animals depending on the type of nanoparticles. Toxic effects are shown by ultrafine particles which have granule metric properties the same as nano-particles. These effects may be in many organs of animals and on different clinical and epidemiological applications which are made on humans. IRSST studied with different nanoparticles synthesized for industrial usage, organic and inorganic nanoparticles, quantum dots, nanoshells, nanocapsules, and nanospheres to see the health effects by taking the effects of ultrafine particles as reference. When nanoparticles are applied to the lungs, they have seen that the lungs get affected depending on the high surface-to-mass ratio; they have shown the degree of toxicity is linked to the surface rather than mass.

Usage in other branches:-

Nanoparticles are also used for information technologies, and the main usage area is the storage of information in smaller sizes. So it has been worked on nanoparticles to produce nanopens and by using photonic crystals chemical/ optical computers have been developed. Quantum (molecular) electronic devices are also still in use as nanoparticle technology examples. Using the flexibility of these materials they are used for replacing metals. Moreover, their hardness is also used instead of metals. By using these metal nanoparticles, it can also be made long-life batteries. In nanotechnology points, they are used for creating unusual colors, and also some of these points have a specialty, self-cleaning.

In environmental applications, nanoparticles are used in solar cells, photo-remediation the destructive absorbents. They can be used as more effective catalysts in chemical applications. Solar heat is reflected in summer and conducted in winter by the nanoparticles also called intelligent nano coating used for windows.

Morphology of nanoparticles:-

In the literature, Nanospheres, nano reefs, nano boxes, and more have appeared. As an effect of a directing or tinplating agent, these morphologies sometimes arise spontaneously. Many of these morphologies are used for some purpose and objective.

Due to their microstructural isotropy, a spherical shape is adopted by amorphous particles. On the other hand, the shape is an isotropy of microcrystalline whiskers depending on their crystal habits. Nanoparticles are sometimes called clusters at the small end of their size range. A few shapes that have grown include spheres, rods, fibers, and cups.

CHAPTER IV

NANOMATERIALS

Introduction:-

The cornerstones of science and nanotechnology are nanomaterials. In the past few years, nanostructures science and technology have grown very rapidly in the whole world. Development and research activity is a broad and interdisciplinary area. Nanoparticles have revolutionized how products and materials are produced and the nature and range of functionalities are accessed. It has important commercial effects which will enhance in the future.

Nanomaterials and technology applications being performed by the nano and advanced materials are described in the article. The importance of nanotechnology is increased by its applications in many fields and areas. It seems that few areas of human technology are exempt from the advantages that nanotechnology brings with it. Practical nanotechnology is based on manipulating matter on small scales which represents possibilities that one could never imagine.

The extraordinary properties of nanomaterials have been exploited for many applications by the biological and medical research communities. In both Vivo and in vitro biomedical research and uses, nanomaterials can be useful. Identification of five focused market sectors has been done. These areas involve sustainable energy, play, and solid-state lighting, construction materials, environmental techniques, and health and medical care products. These sectors were identified where nanomaterials and technologies can add important value and surround the Pearl River Delta region. Description of applications research undertaken by the nano and advanced materials will be given commercializing the. Innovative products are the ultimate objective of this research.

To conduct market-driven applications research of nanomaterials and technology, the Hong Kong university of science and technology was set up in 2006. Its objective was also to develop in Hong Kong that can lead to a wide spectrum of innovative products. There are many nanotechnology products concerned with energy. But most advanced products include: storing conversing by decreasing materials and increasing the use of renewable energy resources. A better insulation system can help in decreasing energy consumption. This can be made possible by the use of lighter and stronger efficient lighting or combustion systems. In heavy industry, there is the inevitable use of nanotechnology. The performance of aircraft manufacturers can be increased by using lighter and stronger materials. due to this, there is a great benefit to space aircraft also as in space aircraft, weight is a major factor. In the nano and advanced materials technology roadmap, five key market areas are targeted.

They include:-

1. *Sustainable energy*
2. *Building/ Construction materials*
3. *Display and solid-state lighting*
4. *Environmental technologies*
5. *Medical and healthcare products*

In the PRD region or area, these are the biggest or largest market sectors. In many fields or areas, the highlights of nano and advanced materials key technologies will be discussed. It can't be believed that the dimensions of nanoscale materials are very less than the diameter of human hair. Dimensions of nanoscale materials are less than ten lakhs smaller than a human hair diameter. Unique optical, electrical, and magnetic, properties emerge at this scale. These properties have such impacts in medicine, electronics, and other fields. If the particles are in the form of an unbound state or as an aggregate or as an agglomerate, any manufactured materials have a size range of 1-100nm.

Nanoparticles have revolutionized how products and materials are produced and the nature and range of functionalities are accessed. It has important commercial effects which will enhance in the future. Regardless of its size, bulk materials should have constant physical properties often observed at the nanoscale size. The percentage of atoms at the surface is significant about the no. of atoms in the bulk of materials larger than one micrometer.

It will be introducing the nanomaterials fullerene, carbon nanotubes, and other materials and applications discussed. Materials referred to as nanomaterials generally fall into two categories. Fullerene and inorganic nanoparticles. Nanoparticles are very useful in packaging, cosmetics, and coatings due to their property of transparency which is rendered to them when they have dimensions below the wavelengths of light. If we try to understand only the influence of nanoparticles on surface atoms then we can't simply predict their properties.

We can define nanoscale as less than one-tenth of a micrometer b. but sometimes, nanoscale is also used for materials smaller than one micrometer. Many naturally occurring nanomaterials are used in or designed for many commercial processes and products. We can find them in sporting goods, cosmetics, sunscreens, tires, electronics, stain-resistant clothing, and in many other items of daily use. For imaging, diagnosis, and in drug delivery, nanomaterials are used in medicine.

The resources are called engineered nanomaterials if they are designed at the molecular level so that advantages of their novel properties and tiny size can be taken, are called engineered nanomaterials. These properties are not present in their bulky and traditional counterparts.

Two main causes of materials having different properties at the nanoscale are increased relative surface area and new quantum effects. Due to their increased greater surface area to volume ratio than their conventional forms, the chemical reactivity and strength of nanomaterials can be influenced. At the nanoscale, the most significant determinant of the characteristics and properties of materials is the quantum effects.

Commercial products available today have a very wide and broad range involving sunscreens, cosmetics, paints, wrinkle-free textiles, stain resistance, etc. many consumer products like sports equipment, automobiles, bicycles, and windows have nanocoatings and nanocomposites. To save beverages or liquid things from damage by sunlight, glass bottles have UV- blocking coatings of nanomaterials.

History of nanomaterials:-

When nanostructures were formed in the early materials, the history of nanomaterials began in no time. When humans started the use of fire, nanoscaled smoke particles were formed. Later, other nanostructures like skeletons seashells, etc. evolved. But their scientific story did not begin soon. Colloidal gold particles are the first scientific report which was synthesized by Michael Faraday in 1867.

Nanostructured catalysts have been discovered for over 10 years. In USA and Germany, for rubber reinforcement, precipitated and fumed silica nanoparticles were sold were manufactured in the early 1940s. In daily use consumer products, like dairy coffee creamer, optical fibers, automobile tires and catalyst supports, etc., nanosized amorphous silica particles have many uses.

For magnetic recording, metallic nanopowders were manufactured in the 1960s and 1970s. Buhrmann and Granqvist published nanocrystals that were created from inert gas evaporation technology. Maya blue paint is a nanostructure hybrid material. It has been clarified recently. Studies of true samples from Jaina Island show that the product has been created from clay crystals that are needle-shaped and form 1.4 nm. But it is still unknown where its color originated.

Today a large no. of structural and functional materials use the properties of nanophase engineering. On the formation of separated small clusters which are fused into a bulk-like substance, the formation of nanophase or cluster assembled materials is based.

Properties of nanomaterials:-

Nanomaterials have structural features in between the features of bulk materials and atoms. The properties of most micro-structured materials are similar to the corresponding bulk materials with nanometer dimensions. The nanometer size of the materials is its cause which them:

(1) a large fraction of surface atoms

(2) High surface energy

(3) spatial confinement

(4) decreased imperfections

which are not present in the corresponding bulk materials.

Nanomaterials have a large surface area to volume ratio as they have tiny dimensions that result in more surface-dependent and material properties. When the sizes of nanomaterials are comparable to length, the surface properties of nanomaterials will affect the whole material. This may result in the modification of the properties of bulk materials. For instance, we can use metallic nanoparticles as very active catalysts. sensitivity and sensor selectivity can be increased by chemical sensors of nanoparticles and nanowires.

The Quantum effect is produced due to the spatial confinement and optical properties of materials can be modified if charge carrier density and energy band structure in the materials is modified differently from their bulk. For instance, light-emitting diodes (LED) and lasers from quantum wires and dots are very promising in future optoelectronics. High-density information storage is also a rapidly developing area.

An important determinant of the properties of nanomaterials is the reduced imperfections. The properties of nanomaterials are influenced by increased materials' perfections. Nanomaterials have better mechanical properties of nanomaterials than bulk materials. Carbon nanotubes have well-known mechanical properties. Nanomaterials have many novel properties due to their nanometer size. A lot of novel uses of nanomaterials have been proposed which rose from these novel properties.

Optical properties:-

The optical properties of nanomaterials are one of the most interesting and useful aspects. Laser sensors, phosphors, optical detectors, solar cells, photo catalyzes, photoelectrochemistry, imaging, display, and biomedicine are the uses based on the optical properties of nanomaterials.

The parameter on which the optical properties of nanomaterials depend is the shape, surface features, and other variables including interactions and doping with the surrounding environment. Similarly, the optical properties of metal nanostructures can be affected by shape. By the figure optical properties of nanoparticles, optical features of metal and semiconductor nanoparticles can be exemplified. When an anisotropy is added to the nanoparticles like the growth of nanorods optical properties of nanomaterials are changed.

Electrical properties:-

The fundamentals of electrical conductivity in nanorods and nanotubes, photoconductivity of nanorods, and electrical conductivity of nanocomposites, and carbon nanotubes are discussed in the electrical properties of nanoparticles. Measurement of electric current at a constant applied voltage and mechanical thinning of nanowires is the method to demonstrate the steps in conductance.

An important point described here is that the electrical conductivity of wire becomes smaller as its diameter is reduced. Electric current is transported only on electron wave mode in electricity conductivity carbon nanotubes. The surface of mercury is touched at different times by the carbon nanotubes as their lengths and orientations are different. As result, two sets of information are obtained:

(1) The resistance of different nanotubes

(2) The effect of carbon nanotubes' length on the resistance surface of memory droplets touched by different carbon nanotubes as they have different lengths these things help in the electrical transport.

Mechanical properties:-

In the mechanical properties of nanoparticles bulk metallic and ceramic materials are dealt with. These materials are influenced by porosity, grain size, superplasticity, filled polymer composites, polymer-based nanocomposites filled with platelets, and carbon nanotube-based composites. It is very difficult to create microscopic bodies having high density and a grain size of below 100nm. Hence, it is just a basic interest to discuss the mechanical properties of nanomaterials. Much interaction has been attracted by two materials none of them is produced by sintering and pressing because they will get industrial importance undoubted. These materials are polymers that have plastic-deformed metals and contain nanoparticles to improve their mechanical behavior.

The latter are not considered nanomaterials due to their large grain size. It has been found by studies on the mechanical properties of bulk materials that they are many problems in creating specimens with exactly defined grain sizes and porosities. Hence, for understanding the mechanical properties of these materials, model calculations and molecular dynamic studies are significant. We will get poor and poor properties if particles of the filler and agglomerates get larger and larger. With very high strength and strain, we can create composite fibers by using carbon nanotubes.

Polymers ceramic nanocomposites are the most exciting nanocomposites where the ceramic phase is platelet-shaped. In the structure of our bone, this type of composite is present, where it is made of a few nanometers thick crystallized materials platelets that are bound together with a matrix called collagen.

Magnetic properties:-

When reduced to nano size, the non-magnetic bulk gold and pt become magnetic. Surface atoms are not only differentiated from bulk atoms but also they can be altered by capping the nanoparticles. i.e. by interaction with other chemical species.

On capping with correct molecules, we can alter the physical properties of nanoparticles by using this method. In reality, Ferro-magnetic behavior can be exhibited by no ferromagnetic bulk materials when they are prepared in the nano range. From non-magnet bulk materials, we can get magnetic nanoparticles of Pd, Platinum, and the surprising case of Aluminum. Ferromagnetism arises from the structural changes in PD & PT concerned with side effects.

Classification of nanomaterials:-

Nanomaterials have extremely small sizes of even less than 100 nm. One-dimensional nanomaterials behave like surface films, two-dimensional like fibers or we can say strands and their dimensional nanomaterials behave like particles. They have variable shapes they can be spherical, irregular, or tubular. Forms of their existence may be single, fused, aggregated, or agglomerated. Forms with spherical, tubular, and irregular shapes. Nanotubes, quantum dots, fullerenes, and dendrimers are types of nanomaterials.

Nanomaterials have been used in the field of nanotechnology. Normal chemicals show different physical, chemicals, for example, silver nanotubes, etc. Nanomaterials have either dimensions of up to 50 nm or have an ultrafine grain size. Richard W. Siegel demonstrated that nanomaterials can be created by many modulation dimensionalities.

Various physical forms in which an element can exist are called allotropes of that element carbon element has a valance of 4. It is tetravalent due to which it is capable of forming various allotropes. Common allotropes of carbon include diamond and graphite. These are well known to us. We are familiar with their structures and properties.

Many allotropes of carbons have been discovered and found recently. These include ball-shaped buckminsterfullerene and sheet-like graphene. Nanobuds, nanotubes, and nanoribbons are larger-scale structures of carbon. Many forms of carbon are capable of exiting at extremely high temperatures or very high pressure. These are unusual forms of carbon. Allotropes of carbon differ in their physical properties due to different arrangements of carbon atoms in them. But they are similar in their chemical properties.

Diamond:-

Diamond is a colorless transparent substance with extraordinary brilliance. It is a well-known allotrope of carbon. Diamond is a substance with excellent physical properties. Most of these properties come in diamonds due to strong covalent bonds between carbon atoms. Diamond has many useful properties due to which it is used in many spheres. It has high heat conductivity. It also has the property of high dispersion of light. Structure of diamond crystal tetrahedral.

They have strong covalent bonds between them. This provides a diamond with a rigid structure. Due to these properties, diamond is the hardest substance present on earth. There is no other harder substance present on earth than diamond. It is used in industrial activities as well as in jewelry making. It has a great ability to hold polish and luster. Diamonds can be found in many colors yellow, blue, brown, green, purple, pink, orange, or red.

Industrial-grade diamonds are very different from gem-grade diamonds. Diamonds are used in industries due to their hardness and heat conductivity but they are used in gem making for their clarity and color. 80% of mined diamonds are used for industrial purposes. They are not suitable for use as gemstones and are called booty. Recently synthetic diamonds are replacing natural diamonds.

History of diamonds:-

The name diamond has been derived from the ancient Greek word which means proper, unbreakable, and untamed. Diamonds have been known in India for at least 3000 years. They are thought to have been first recognized and mined in India. They were probably found in alluvial deposits of the stone along the rivers Penne, Krishna, and Godavari. The popularity of diamonds has risen since the 19th century.

In ancient India, diamonds were used as religious icons. Different experiments have been carried out to prove that diamond is composed of carbon. Diamond is made only of CO_2. This has been demonstrated in 1772 by

Antoine Lavoisier. He used a convex lens and concentrated the sun's rays on diamonds. He covered ut this demonstration in the presence of oxygen.

He found the only product formed after combustion was Smitson Tennant stated that the burning of diamonds released a gas that turned lime water milky. Then it was proved that the gas is carbon dioxide because only carbon dioxide turns lime water milky. This established the chemical equivalence of these substances. Four features or characteristics, informally known as the four C_S, are used as basic descriptors of diamonds. These characteristics are carat, cut, color, and clarity. A large, flawless diamond is known as a paragon.

Metallic properties of diamond:-

Hardness:-

Since ancient times, the hardness of diamonds is known. its hardness can be demonstrated on the Mobs scale. On this scale, hardness is described as a resistance to scratching. It is graded between 1to 10. The hardness of a diamond is on a 10 Mobs scale of mineral hardness.

Diamond is even suitable for daily wear due to its high resistance to scratching. It is worn by ladies in rings, earrings, and other ornaments. It has extraordinary shine also. In engagement and marriage rings, its popularity has been enhancing cope ton and Bingers area in New South Wales in Australia. From these regions, natural diamonds originated mostly.

Electrical conductivity:-

Diamonds do not conduct electricity. They differ in this property from graphite. Diamonds do not conduct electricity due to the absence of free ions in them. Due to this, diamonds are used as excellent electrical insulators. In a diamond crystal, each carbon atom is joined to four other carbon atoms. So, all 4 valance electrons of each carbon atom are used in bond formation.

Due to this, a diamond has no free electrons and does not conduct electricity. Some blue diamonds are natural semiconductors also. Boron impurity gives rise to this blue color and conductivity.

Graphite:-

Abraham Got lob Werner named it in 1789. It is chemically similar to diamond but the arrangement of carbon atoms is different in graphite. In graphite one carbon atom is joined to three other carbon atoms. Carbon atoms form a layer or sheet in graphite. But layers of carbon atoms in graphite are apart such that nee covalent bonding can exist between them. They are joined by Vander Waals forces which are very weak.

Graphite has a sheet-like structure due to which it is a soft substance. Unlike diamond, Graphite is a good conductor of electricity. We know that carbon has a valiancy of four. Now, in Graphite each carbon atom is joined to three other carbon atoms. So, only 3 valence electrons of each carbon atom are used in bond formation. The fourth electron is free to move. So, due to the presence of free electrons, Graphite conducts electricity. Under standard conditions and situations, graphite is the most stable form of carbon. In electrical arc lamp electrodes, graphite can be used.

Graphite is used in thermochemistry to define the heat of the formation of carbon compounds. Due to the delocalization of pi bonds electrons above and below the planes of carbon atoms, graphite conducts electrical energy. But it does not conduct electricity at right angles to the plane. Due to its softness, graphite is used in lubricating any machine parts.

So, it can be used to lubricate those machine parts which operate at a very high temperature. To be used as a lubricant, graphite can be made into powder or mixed with petroleum jelly. In a vacuum, graphite behaves as a very poor lubricant. due to this fact, it was established that the lubricity of graphite is because of absorbed water and air between the layers. It has been suggested or proposed by recent studies that an effect known as superlubricity can also cause this effect. In blood-contracting implants like prosthetic heart values, a paralytic carbon is a useful substance. When a large number of crystalloid graphic defects bind planes of graphite together then graphite loses its lubrication properties. Natural properties have mainly three types or forms.

Different types of ore deposits contain each type of graphite. These forms include:-

- *Crystalline flake graphite*
- *Amorphous graphite*
- *Lump graphite*

Occurrence:-

Graphite occurs in igneous and metamorphic rocks and meteorites. During metamorphism. It occurs as a result of the reduction of sedimentary carbon compounds in metamorphic rocks. Minerals associated with graphite are calaite, quartz, micas, and tourmaline. It occurs with trotline and silicate minerals in meteorites. Clintonites are small graphitic crystals in meteoritic iron. World production of natural graphite in the year 2012 was 1100 thousand tonnes. This report was given by the United States Geological Survey.

Properties of graphite:-

Alpha and beta are two known forms of graphite. They show resemblance in their physical properties. Through mechanical treatments, alpha can be changed into beta. When beta is heated above 1300° C it converts into alpha. Due to the vast delocalization of electrons in carbon layers, graphite is a good conductor of electricity. In early carbon microphones, powered graphite is used as a semiconductor substitute. This is due to the conductive properties of graphite.

Uses of natural graphite:-

Graphite has the following main uses:-

A. Batteries:-

In the construction of the anode of all major battery technologies, graphite is used. For this purpose, we can use both natural and artificial graphite. In the last 30 years, its use in batteries has been increasing. Lithium carbonate uses less amount of graphite than lithium-ion batteries. Lithium carbonate battery uses two times less amount of graphite than a lithium-ion battery. Graphite demand experienced growth in the late1980s and early 1990 due to the increase in the demand for batteries mainly nickel-metal-hydride and lithium-ion batteries.

The demand for batteries has been enhanced due to laptops, mobile phones, tablets, and smartphone products. Graphite demand has been increased by electric vehicle batteries also. For instance, a fully electric Nissan Leaf contains a lithium-ion battery that has nearly 40kg of graphite. So, the use of graphite in batteries cannot be overlooked.

B. Steel making:

Graphite has important industrial applications in steel making. The dies used for extruding hot steel are lubricated using graphite. To enhance the carbon content of the steel to the specified level, a carbon raiser is added. It has been indicated by a survey that 10,500 tonnes of graphite were used in the fashion in 2005.

C. Pencils:-

The word graphite has been derived from the Greek word graphing which means to write or to draw. Graphite can leave marks on paper and other objects. Due to this property, graphite is used in pencil leads. For this purpose, a mixture of clay and powdered graphite is used in pencil leads. In 1795, Nicholas- Jacques Conte invented the pencil lead. Plumb ago is another older term used for natural graphite. This term was used mainly in 17th and 18th-century works. In 2011, around 790 of 1.1 million tones of graphite produced were used to make pencils. From china low Quality amorphous graphite is used and sourced. We can conclude that at present, important markets for natural graphite are pencils though they are small.

D. Other uses:-

Despite these uses, graphite is used in many materials. It is used in electric motor brushes, zinc-carbon batteries, foundry facings, and refractory's. It has many other specialized applications. To form a heat-resistant protective coating for the exposed portions of a steam locomotive boiler, powdered graphite is of ten mixed with waste oil by railroads.

Difference between diamond and graphite:-

Two materials made of the same element can be more different than graphite and diamond or more extreme in their differences. Diamond is one of the hardest materials while graphite is the softest. As a result, diamond is used as an abrasive, and graphite is used as a lubricant (interestingly, graphite has recently been shown to be a poor lubricant in space. Diamond is also a lubricant that is used in the space shuttle on bearings. Graphite is electrically conducting and diamond is electrically insulating; however, a diamond can be made semiconducting by adding dopants (p-doping only).

Diamond is optically transparent and graphite is optically dense. Diamond crystallites are members of the isometric (cubic) system; graphite crystals are members of the hexagonal system. Diamond has an isotropic structure, whereas graphite structure is anisotropic. Diamond conducts heat extremely well (one of the best in that capacity), but graphite, taken as a whole, does not (graphite conducts heat very well "in the plane"; inter-plane conduction graphite is poor). Interestingly, graphite is the stable form of the two. Diamond is constantly undergoing transition into graphite, albeit quite slowly, the activation energy for this conversion is nearly equal to the lattice energy of a diamond. The fact that diamond was made of carbon was verified in 1796.

The best allotrope of carbon is Diamond which is the hardest known material in the world. It is used both in jewelry and industry due to its hardness and high light dispersion. It can hold luster and polish very well. All its properties make it an excellent abrasive. Its hardness can be judged by the fact that any naturally occurring substance has no potential to cut a diamond.

The most important feature of diamond used by industries is its high heat conductivity and hardness, making a lot of gemological features of a diamond, involving, color and clarity, mainly irrelevant. Now we can understand why 80 % of mined diamonds that are unsuitable are used as gemstones and also called bort, are regarded as gold for industrial use.

Synthetic and mined in the 1950s and immediately, they were put to industrial use. 400 million creates synthetic diamonds are produced for industrial use every year. Diamonds are mostly and dominantly used in grinding, cutting, polishing, and drilling. Large diamonds are not used in these techniques. Gem-quality diamonds are mostly used in industries.

Special uses of diamonds are in science laboratories where they are used in high-performance bearings, and high-pressure experiments and also have limited and restricted use in specialized windows. Many advances have been achieved in the production of synthetic diamonds. As a result, future uses will become more efficient and easily feasible. Diamonds can be used as a semiconductor to make and produce microchips or diamonds can be used as a heat sink in electronics.

Due to diamonds' unique material properties, researches are underway in Europe, Japan, and the United States to capitalize on its potential along with enhanced quantity and quality of supply. Each carbon atom in a diamond forms four bonds with other carbons in a tetrahedron. A 3-dimensional network of six-numbered carbon rings is formed by these tetrahedrons. The other most common allotrope of carbon is graphite. Graphite is a good conductor of electricity. Thus in electrical arc lamp electrodes, it can be used. The most stable form of carbon is graphite. Hence, thermochemistry is used for explaining the heat of the formation of carbon compounds. Because of the delocalization of pi-bond electrons above and below the planes of carbon atoms, graphite conducts electricity.

All four outer electrons of each carbon atom in the diamond are localized between the atoms in covalent bonding. Diamond does not conduct electricity due to the absence of free electron flow. On the other hand in graphite, each atom of carbon utilizes only three out of four energy shells of electrons in covalent bonding to three other carbon atoms. To a delocalized system of electrons, one electron is contributed by each carbon. The delocalized electrons are freely moving electrons in the plane. As a result, electricity is conducted by the graphite but needs at right angles to the plane.

Graphite powder is used as a dry lubricant. Graphite is a very poor lubricant in a vacuum environment. This led to the invention of the fact that graphite's lubricity is because of the absorbed water and air between the layers. Recently studies have shown that this effect can be accounted for by superlubricity. When a large no. of crystallographic defects binds these planes, useful material called paralytic carbon is formed, and as a result, graphite loses its lubrication properties.

This new material is useful in the blood to contain implants like prosthetic heart valves. For missile nosecones, high-temperature reactors, electric motor brushes, paralytic graphite, and carbon fiber graphite are used. Fitted around the parameter of a fire door, graphites are used in fire seals. During the fire, graphite prevents the spread of fumes by expanding and charring to resist fire penetration. Graphite is lighter than a diamond as its density is only 2.3. Graphite can be changed into diamond at high temperatures and pressure.

It forms CO_2 by burning in oxygen at about 700^0C. As a result, it is more highly reactive than diamond. Ordinary solvents fused alkalis, and dilute acids do not influence it. But it is oxidized to CO_2 by chromic acid. Graphene is a single layer of graphite that has uncommon thermal, physical, and electrical properties. It can be produced by mechanical exfoliation from graphite replacing silicon in high-performance electronic devices is its one application.

Fullerene:-

It is any molecule made wholly of carbon. It can be a hollow sphere, ellipsoid tube, and many other forms. Buckyballs resemble the balls used in footballs and they are spherical fullerenes. On the other hand, cylindrical fullerenes are called buck tubes or carbon non-tubes. The first fullerene named Buckminsterfullerene [C_{60}] was identified and discovered by Richard Smalley, Robert Curll, James Heath, Sean O'Brien, and Harold Crete in 1985. They carried out this research at Rice University.

Buckminster Fuller was named after Buckminster Fuller a famous American Architect. This happened because the structure of Buckminsterfullerene resembled the framework of dome-shaped halls designed by Fuller for large American exhibitions. Earlier, it was assumed that diamond, graphite, and amorphous carbon such as suet and charcoal were the only allotropes of carbon. But now, with the discovery of fullerenes, the no. of carbon allotropes has increased.

Fullerenes have been detected in outer space recently. Intense research has been carried out on buck balls and buck tubes due to their extraordinary and unique chemistry as well as for their technological applications such as materials science, electronics, and nanotechnology.

Types of fullerene:-

There are the following types of fullerene:-

1. *Buck ball clusters*
2. *Nanotubes*
3. *Mega tubes*
4. *Polymers*
5. *Nano "onions"*
6. *Linked "ball-and-chain "dimmers*

7. *Fullerene rings*

Buckyballs:-

A. Buckminster fullerene: -

It can be found in soot. So, it is the most common in terms of natural occurrence. It is also the smallest fullerene molecule that contains pentagonal and hexagonal rings. Buckminsterfullerene consists of 60 carbon atoms joined together to form spherical molecules. Its formula is C_{60}. It is made of 20 hexagons and 12 pentagons. It resembles football in structure. The C_{60} Molecule has two bond lengths. Its average bond length is 1.4 angstroms.

B. Carbon nanotubes:-

Carbon nanotubes are cylindrical fullerenes. Their diameter is about a few nanometers. Their ends may be closed or open. Their ends may be closed or open. Their extraordinary properties involve high tensile strengths, high conductivity, and relative chemical inactivity. To produce high tensile carbon cables required by a space elevator, they are used in paper batteries and the field of space technologies.

Properties of fullerene:-

The physical and chemical properties of fullerenes have been a hot topic in the field of research and development. Due to their unusual properties, fullerenes are used in many fields.

A. Aromaticity:-

It has been found that if active groups are attached to the surfaces of fullerenes then their reactivity increases. Researchers have been able to discover this. Superaromaticity means that the electrons in the hexagonal rings do not delocalize over the whole surface. Buckminsterfullerene does not exhibit this property. They should try to delocalize the whole molecule.

B. Solubility:-

There are many solvents in which fullerenes are sparingly soluble. Common solvents involve aromatics like toluene and others such as carbon disulfide. Purple color has been observed in the solutions of pure buckminsterfullerene. On the other hand, solutions of C_{70} are reddish brown. At room temperature, fullerenes can be dissolved in common solvents.

They are the only allotropes of carbon that have these properties. Small fullerenes such as C_{28}, C_{36}, and C_{50} are not soluble in solvents because they have small band gaps between the ground and excited states. These small band gap fullerenes are very reactive.

The name fullerene was used for the family of fullerenes as the fullerene family was discovered after the buckminsterfullerene. The indication of the covalently bonding of each carbon atom to three others is represented by the suffix "ene". The unique C_{20} is the smallest fullerene. There are no known fullerenes that have 22 vertices. Researchers at Virginia Tech invented the trimester sphere carbon nanomaterials. So carbon atoms are comprised in this class of novel molecules and create a sphere that encloses a complex of their metal atoms and one nitrogen atom. Trimetaaspheres can be used in diagnostics.

Carbon nanotubes:-

Their nanotubes have a named structure of cylindrical shape. With a length-to-diameter ratio of up to 132,0000,000:1, which is importantly larger than any other material, nanotubes have been formed. Because of their mechanical and electrical properties and unusual heat conductivity, carbon nanotubes are used as additives for many structural materials. For instance, in baseball bats, golf clubs, or car parts nanotubes form a small portion of materials.

Nanotubes are the meembers of fullerene structural family. Nanotubes' name is taken from hollow and ling structure which is created from graphene. At specific and discrete angles, these sheets are rolled and nanotube properties are decided by the combination of radius and rolling angle. For instance, individual nanotube shells in semiconductors or a metal.

We can categorize the nanotubes as multi-walled nanotubes and single-walled nanotubes. Chemical bonding in nanotubes is described by orbital hybridization. Sp^2 bonds, similar to graphite together compose the chemical bonding of nanotubes get, andunique strength due to these bonds is found in diamond and alkenes and is stronger.

Types of carbon nanotubes:-

Single-Walled carboon nanotubes:-

Single-walled carbon nanotubes have millions of times longer tubes and about 1 nm diameter. The way a graphene sheet is wrapped can be represented by using a pair of indices. Integer n and m denote the numbers of unit vectors along the two directions in the honeycomb crystals lattice of graphene nanotubes are called the armchair nanotubes.

Most of the properties of SWNTs alter with the nm values and this dependence is non-monotonic. So SWNTs are significant types of carbon nanotubes. Metallic or semiconducting behavior can be represented by their electrical conductivity. Particularly, their band gap varies from 0 to 2 eV. The structure of SWNTs is represented in fig 4.10. The candidates too miniature electronics are single-walled nanotubes. The most basic building block of these systems is the electric wire. SWNTs with a diameter of nanometers can prove to be better conductors

Developing the first intermolecular field effect transistors (FET) is one useful application of SWNTs. In 2001, the first intermolecular logic gate was made using SWCNT FETs. Both p-FET and n-FET are needed to make a logic gate. Half of S WNT exposed to oxygen can be saved when SWNT p-FET and n-FETs while exposing the other half part to oxygen. It results in a single SWNT that acts as a NOT logic gate with both p and n-type FETs within the same molecule.

Multi-Walled carbon nanotubes:-

MWNT has multiple rolled layers of graphene. To describe the structure of multi-walled nanotubes, these are two models. These are the Russian Doll model and the Parchment model. Graphite sheets are arranged in econometric cylinders in the Russian Doll model.

In the parchment model, a single graphite sheet is rolled around itself like a rolled newspaper. We can observe a Russian Doll structure. We can describe SWNTs as individual shells which can be semiconducting or metallic. Due to the statistical possibilities and restrictions on the relative diameters of the individual tubes the whole MWNT is a zero-zero gap metal.

Properties of carbon nanotubes:-

1. Strength:-

Carbon nanotubes have great tensile strength and elastic modules. They are very strong and are known to have great stiffness. Carbon nanotubes have very strong covalent sp^2 bonds. The covalent sp^2 is performed between the individual carbon atoms. The tensile strength of multi-walled carbon nanotubes in 2000 is 63 Giga pascals.

Carbon nanotubes have a low density for the solid. Its unique strength of up to 48,000 $km.kg^{-1}$ is among many materials. The tubes will undergo permanent plastic deformation under extreme tensile strain. The start of deformation takes place at 5% strains. The strength of multi-walled carbon nanotubes decreases effectively due to weak shear interactions between advancement shells and tubes. Recently high-energy electron irradiations which cross-link inner tubes and shells addressed this limitation. The strength of materials enhances to 60 GPA effectively for multi-walled carbon nanotubes and those of doubled-walled carbon nanotubes increase to 17 GPA.

But under compression CNTs are not so strong. When placed under bending compressive and torsion stress, they undergo buckling and hollow structure ratio. Axial properties of nanotubes are referred to by the above debate while it has been suggested by simple geometrical considerations suggest that carbon nanotubes should be much softer in the radial direction along the tube axis.

In reality, two adjacent tubes can be deformed by even Vander walls forces. This has been proposed by radial elasticity of TEM observation. CNTs are soft in the radial direction. This has been indicated by Nanoindentation experiments on multi-walled carbon nanotubes and tapping mode atomic force microscope measurements performed on single-walled carbon nanotube

2. Hardness:-

Without showing deformation single-walled carbon nanotubes can tolerate about 24 GPA pressure. They can be altered into super hard phase nanotubes. The maximum pressure measured using the current experimental technique is 55GPA. If albeit and higher pressure is applied to these new super hard nanotubes then they can even collapse under high pressure and temperature, graphite can be changed into a diamond which is the hardest known material in the world.

When SWNT is compressed to 24 GPA or above at room temperature, then super hard material can be synthesized. The hardness of these materials is 62-152 GPA as measured in nanoindenters. Diamond is 150 GPA harder while the boron nitride sample is 62 GPA harder. Super hard phase nanotubes have a bulk modulus of 462-546 GPA which is even higher than diamond. Every single crystal of diamond has a hardness of about 420 GPA.

3. Kinetic properties:-

We can call multiple concentric nanotubes multi-walled nanotubes that are nested within one another. A stinking telescoping property is exhibited by them whereby without any friction, the inner nanotube core can slide within its outer nanotube shell. This results in examples of molecular nanotechnology and this characteristic have been used for producing the smallest rotational motor in the world. Gigahertz mechanical oscillator which is one of the future applications is also envisaged.

4. Electrical properties:-

Because of the unique electrical structure and symmetry of graphene electrical properties of nanotubes are affected. If n is equal to m, the nanotubes are metallic, and if n is equal to m is a multiple of or it is semiconducting with little band gap otherwise it is a moderate semiconductor. It states that all armchair nanotubes are metallic.

Theoretically metallic tubes have the potential to conduct a current density of 4 × 108 A/cm^2, which is 1000 times more than metals like copper. Electrons *propagate along the tube's axis because of their nanoscale cross-section. Quantum effects are included in electron transport. Due to this, carbon nanotubes can be referred to as one-dimensional conductors. $2G_0$ is the maximum electrical conductance of a single-walled carbon nanotube where $G_0=2e^2/h$ is the conductance of the ballistic quantum channel. Multi-walled carbon nanotubes interconnected with inner shells show superconductivity with Tc=12k. In contrast, the value is an order of magnitude lower for ropes of single-walled carbon nanotubes than for MWNTS with usual shells that are not inter-connected.*

5. Thermal properties:-

Nanotubes are known to have good thermal conductivity. They exhibit a property called "ballistic conduction". It has been resulted by measurements that an SWNT has a thermal conductivity of nearly 3500 $W{\cdot}m^{-1}{\cdot}K^{-1}$; at room temperature along its axis as compared to copper. An SWNT exhibits a thermal conductivity of near about 1.51 $W{\cdot}m^{-1}{\cdot}K^{-1}$, at room temperature which represents that it is thermally conductive as soil. In a vacuum, Carbon nanotubes have temperature stability of nearly 2800 °C and near about 750 °C in air.

Potential and current applications of carbon nanotubes:-

Platinum catalysis can be replaced by nanotubes to decrease oxygen in fuel cells. Applications and current use of nanotubes can be reduced by vertically aligned nanotubes. A tensile strength similar to individual tubes can't be achieved by bulk nanotube materials. Bulk carbon nanotubes as being used in the polymer as composite fibers. Composite fibers improve the thermal, electrical, and mechanical properties of bulk products. As we know that bulk nanotubes can't achieve the strength as that of individual tubes. However, the strength required for many applications can be yielded by these composites. Bulk carbon nanotubes have the following properties and applications.

1.Structural:-

Many structures, ranging from daily-use items like clothes and sports gear, have been proposed by the mechanical properties of carbon nanotubes. Nevertheless to refine carbon nanotubes technology space elevator is needed. Outstanding breakthroughs have been made for perspective. It has been shown by Ray H. Baughman that materials with toughness not matched with the natural and manmade worlds can be created by single and multi-walled carbon nanotubes.

For producing bulletproof and stabproof clothes, researchers are underway to weave carbon nanotubes into clothes due to their extreme mechanical strength.

The kinetic energy of bullets can lead the damage to bones and internal bleeding. The carbon nanotubes have the potential to stop the bullet from penetrating the body.

2. In electrical circuits:-

Nanotube-based transistors also called carbon nanotube field effect transistors (CNT FETs) use a single electron for digital switching. Due to the lack of technology for mass production, the realization of nanotubes is very difficult. A method as defined by IBM researchers in 2001 to ruin metallic nanotubes while semi-conducting nano-tubes were left behind to be used as transistors. Constructive destruction is the creation of automatic destruction of defective nanotubes on the wafer.

But only electrical properties can be controlled by this process. The potential of carbon nanotubes was demonstrated in 2003. Ohmic metal contact formation was a topic challenge at that time. As a result, Schottky barrier-free contacts were exhibited to semiconductive nanotubes with a diameter greater than 1.7 nm by a high-work function metal called palladium. Firs integrated memory circuit of nanotubes was made in 2004. Regulation of the conductivity of nanotubes is one of the main challenges. Nanotubes can conduct as a semiconductor depending on suitable surface features. An entirely automated way has been evolved to replace nonsemiconductor tubes.

By utilizing their random networks, we can produce carbon nanotube transistors. By doing so large-scale devices can be created at the wafer level. This approach was first patented by nano mix Inc. It was first published by United States Naval Research Laboratory in academic literature in 2003 by independent research using this approach, Nanomix made the first transition on a transparent and flexible substrate. Large structures of carbon nanotubes can be used for the thermal management of electronic circuits about 1mm thick layer of carbon nanotubes was utilized to fabricate coolers. It is a material having very less density. It has 20 times less weight than copper having the same structure. But both materials have the same cooling properties.

3.Paper batteries:-

The paper battery uses a single sheet of cellulose which is then like paper and infused with carbon nanotubes. Nanotubes behave like electrodes which allow the storage devices to conduct electric current. Ling and speedy power output can be as compared to the traditional battery can be provided by the paper battery which performs the functions of both supercapacitor and lithium-ion battery. All of the battery components can be integrated by the paper battery into a single structure. This makes the battery more energy efficient.

4.Solar cells:-

Due to their strong UV absorption properties single-walled carbon nanotubes are used in solar panels. It is one of the most promising applications. Even in their unoptimized state, these tubes can give a sizeable increase in feasibly and efficiency as shown by research. The carbon nanotube complex, created by a mixture of carbon nanotubes and carbon Buckyballs is used in solar cells which were invented at the New Jersey Institute of technology. The function of buckyballs is to trap electrons.

Electrons can't be made to flow by them, when sunlight is added to the polymers, electrons are grabbled by buckyballs. Nanotubes can be able to make the current flow if they start behaving like copper wires. Additional research has been done for enhancing efficiency further and producing SWNT hybrid solar panels. By combing SWNTs with photo-excitable electron donors, these hybrids can be produced. This would enhance the no. of electrons generated. Electro-hole pairs are generated by the interactions between photo-excited porphyry and SWNT. Due to this phenomenon, efficiency can be increased up to 8.5%. This has been observed experimentally.

5. Ultracapacitors:-

Nanotubes are used to improve ultracapacitors by the MIT Laboratory for electromagnetic and electronic systems. Conventional ultracapacitors, which used activated charcoal, have a lot of tiny hollow sources of various sizes. Ultracapacitors create a large surface area for storing electric charge. A significant fraction of the electrode surface is not available as the hollow spaces are not compatible with charge requirements. With a nanotube electrode, the spaces may be tailored to size-some too small and some too large and consequently the ability should be increased considerably.

6.Medical:-

In the cancerous cells, carbon nanotubes are inserted during the Kanzius cells during the Kanzis cancer therapy. Then by using radio waves, these cells can be heated up and then killed. It has been represented by researchers at Rice University, University of California, Nijmegen Medical center, and Redbud University that carbon nanotubes are suitable for the proliferation of bone cells and bone formation.

7.Textile:-

On fiber spinning the studies on the utilization of CNTs in textile fictionalization focus so how mechanical and physical properties can be improved. In recent times more focus is on coating CNTs on textile fabrics. To modify fabrics with CNTs, various methods have been developed. Intelligent textiles have been created by Shim et al. for human bio-monitoring using a polyelectrolyte-based coating with CNTs. Single-walled carbon nanotubes were coated with a simple dipping and drying process for wearable electronic and energy storage uses by Hu and his colleagues. CNTs have a negative electric charge and aligned nanotube structure. The exhaustion method is applied on the fiber surface for coating and absorbing CNTs. This will help to prepare multi-functional fabric involving electric conductive and electromagnetic properties.

8. Other applications:-

In nanoelectromechanical systems, like nanoscale electric motors and mechanical memory elements, carbon nanotubes have been implemented. A hydrogen sensor was developed by nano mix inc. in May 2005 and integrated carbon nanotubes on a silicon platform. For high-reliability touch screens and flexible displays, carbon nanotubes are ideal as they are more mechanically robust than ITO films. A radio receiver was demonstrated in 2007 that was made of a single nanotube called a nano radio. It answers represents in 2008 that applying an alternating current, a sheet of nanotubes can work like a loudspeaker. The sound is created by thermo acoustically rather than by vibration.

The electric grid can become efficient by storing electricity and many power suppliers like wind turbines can meet their energy needs because energy can be removed from or added to flywheels very efficiently but everything depends on the cost of making. Unbroken and massive structures of nanotubes. Elastic potential energy can be stored in carbon nanotubes. For delivering MRI contrast agents in vivo short SWNTs have been utilized as nanoscaled capsules. Carbon nanotubes have provided the potential for metal-free catalysis of organic or inorganic. For example, oxygen groups attached to the surface of carbon nanotubes can catalyze selective oxidation. In preventing carbon nano oxide poisoning nanotubes also have been successful.

CHAPTER V

APPLICATIONS OF NANOTECHNOLOGY

Introduction:-

When the future sizes were shrunk then a lot of improved products and materials depend on changes in the physical properties. Due to their increased surface area-to-volume ratio, nanoparticles have many advantages. Fluorescence is included in the example of optical properties of nanomaterials that become a function of the particle diameter. Mechanical properties of the material like elasticity or stiffness are influenced when nanoparticles are brought into a bulk material. For example, nanoparticles can reinforce conventional polymers that result in novel properties that can be utilized as lightweight replacements for metals. Nevertheless, an enhancing societal advantage of such nanoparticles can be expected.

With an increase in stability and improved functionality, weight reduction has been enabled in such nanotechnology-enhanced materials. For providing advantages to society, applications of nanotechnology are provided in unexpected and expected ways. This is happening after more than 20 years of basic nanoscience research and 10 years of focused R & D under NNI. Industrial sector information techniques environmental science, homeland securing, medicine, food safety, and transportation have improved as well as been revolutionized by nanotechnology. A list of applications and advantages of nanotechnology are described below. Many advantages of nanotechnology rely on this fact. Materials can be made lighter, more durable, stronger, more reactive, and better electrical conductors by using the applications of nanotechnology.

Medical and health applications:-

Unique properties of nanomaterials from many uses have been exploited by the medical and biological research communities. This hybrid field can be illustrated by the terms like nanobiotechnology, nanomedicine, and biomedical nanotechnology. By interfacing nanomaterials with biological structures, functionalities can be added to them. Nanomedicine has played a vital role in preventing illness, diagnosing, treating, and trauma of reliving pain, and for preserving. Using genetic engineering, nanoscale structured materials, biotechnology, and evenly complex machine system and nanorobots. It should become possible to make up parts on the nanometer scale by constructing machines on the micrometer scale within 15-20 years. For molecule-by-molecule regent purification and smooth super hard surfaces, automatically flawless diamonds are present in 10nm tiny robots. Nanomechanical devices will be controlled activated and deactivated using nanocomputers. External signals and stimuli will be proceeded by nanocomputers and they will store and execute mission plans, and the nanocomputer. His technology has enormous dental and medical applications. Precise intervention at the cellular and molecular level would be performed by a physician with programmable nanorobotics devices. For clinical diagnosis, medical nanorobots have been proposed. Nanotechnology has been used in clinical diagnosis, dentistry, mechanically reversing atherosclerosis, etc. It also improves the respiratory capacity, enabling near instantaneous homeostasis, supplementing the immune system by rewriting or replacing DNA sequences in cells, repairing brain damage, and resolving a gross cellular insult and in pharmaceutical research.

Diagnostics:-

Nanotechnology is used in laboratories for diagnostic purposes. For example magnetic nanoparticles with bound to a suitable antigen. The properties of magnetic nanoparticles get used to label specific molecules, and microorganisms and also use for the detection of a genetic sequence. For analysis of nucleic acids that converts strings of nuclei acids into an electronic signature for their used nanopore four technologies.

Drug delivery:-

Nanotechnology is also used in Drug delivery in India. In the following field cardiology, ophthalmology, endocrinology, immunology, oncology, and stem cell research is advancing in India because nanotechnology is used in this research and is very important. Costs and human suffering have been covered by this selective approach. Micelles are formed by co-polymers, for drug encapsulation by these small drug molecules that are transported to the desired location. Some other necessary applications involve the treatment of cancer using gold shells and iron nanoparticles. In both in vitro and in vivo biomedical research and application, nanomaterials are successful. The size of nanomaterials is the same as that of biological molecules and structures. Diagnostic devices, analytical instruments, physical therapy, drug-transferring vehicles, and applications can be developed by the integration of nanomaterials with biology.

Tissue engineering:-

Damaged tissues can be repaired or reproduced by nanotechnology. Artificially stimulated cell proliferation can be used by tissue engineering. Today's traditional systems such as artificial implants and organ transplants might be replaced by tissue engineering. For transplantation and expansion into the ECM, there may not be enough healthy cells for patients with end-stage organ failure. Pluripotent stem cells are required if a such thing occurs. These cells have the benefit of avoiding rejection. These ordinary cells are programmed into a pluripotent stage and are taken from the patient's own body. Embryos used as another potential source of pluripotent cells have two following disadvantages.

1.) This process needs the harvesting of embryos. As a result, this source is considered ethically problematic.

2.) The problem of closing which is technically very different needs to be solved.

Nanorobotic microbivores:-

Phagocytes present in blood that digesting unwanted pathogens like bacteria, viruses, fungi, and foreign bodies. Artificial paginates developed known as micro bivalves. Artificial phagocytes also do the same function in our blood as human original phagocytes seeking out and digesting unlike diseases causing germs such as bacteria, viruses, or fungi.

Surgical nanorobotics:-

A surgical nanorobot was used for surgery by a human surgeon. When nanorobots are introduced into the human body through cavities of the vascular system then they act as semiautonomous onsite surgeons inside the body. Such a device that involves searching for pathology, then treatment, and then treating by ion present at the morbid area by nanomanipulation has many functions to be performed. Such manipulation has maintained contact with the supervising surgeon by coded ultrasound signals. Micropipette below a one-micrometer tip diameter has been used to completely rely on cut dendrites from signal neurons without damage to cell viability. Hence it can be concluded that today, many forms of cellular nanosurgery are being searched. Axons were regenerated after performing taxonomy of roundworms neurons laser surgery. Femtolaser surgery represented the individual chromosomes. The laser works like a pair of nanoscissors by vaporizing tissue locally on leaving adjacent tissue unharmed.

Nanogenerators:-

Nanogenerators produce electric currents. Polymer-based films can grow nanowires. Nanogenerators could also generate portable electronic energy from muscle stretching, movements of the body, or flow of the water into electricity. These nanogenerators were represented by Wang at PUNC in nanoscience and technology. He states that these nanogenerators can change mechanical energy into electric energy for powering devices in the body.

Nanodentistry:-

By employing nanomaterials, biotechnology, and including tissue engineering and dental nanorobotics, the maintenance of comprehensive oral health can be possible. Local anesthesia, dentition denaturalization, permanent hypersensitivity cure, whole orthodontic realignments, covalently bonded diamondized, and continues oral health maintenance dentist robots are involved n the new potential treatment opportunities in dentistry. Dental nanorobots may use special motility mechanisms. When the first micro-size dental nanorobots can be restructured. This is done to swim or crawl through human tissue with navigational precision. Uses of a multitude of technologies involve monitoring, interrupting, and changing nerve impulse traffic in individual nerve cells in actual time. In response to local sensor stimuli, programmed instruction is executed by nanorobots functions that are controlled by onboard nanocomputers. By transmitting orders directly into Vivo nanorobots by acoustic signals, the dentist may issue strategic instructions.

Inducing anesthesia:-

In dental practice, the most common producers are to make oral anesthesia. After contacting the surface of the mucosa of the crown by passing through lamina propepria, the active analgesic nanorobotics reaches the dent. Nanorobots go inside the dentinal tubule hole after reaching the dent. these holes are processed toward the pulp. The natural cells are continuously moving around and inside the teeth including pulp fibroblasts and human gingival, bacteria inside dentinal tubules, dentin border cement blasts of the CDI, and lymphocytes within the pulp. Nerve impulse traffic was once controlled by nanorobots when they interred in the pulp. In any particular tooth that needs cure when the oral procedure is finished, the sensitivity is shut down on the order of the dentist on analgesic dental nanorobots. All sensations can be restored by decreased curiosity, aspiration no needles, broad selectivity, control ability of analgesic impact, and fast and fully reversible switch.

Molecular motors:-

Different components have to be over within large biological structures like individual cells. Diffusing alone can move ions and molecules including larger biological structures. The diffusion of molecular species becomes less efficient as they become larger. The molecular motor is the most fascinating among these.

During the study of one of the bodies known as potassium, sodium ATPase, the discovery of molecular motors took place. The energy stored in the ATP molecule is produced and transuded by this complex enzyme. The ATP

(Adenosine Tri Phosphate) molecules which store the energy produced by the oxidation of food during respiration, are also known as the energy currency of the cell. Each ATP molecule contains about 30.5 kg of energy. Approximately 38 ATP molecules are produced by the oxidation of 1 molecule of glucose. ATPase works like a rotary motor actually which is the central unit of mono structures. Functional biology of the cell is one of the many molecular motor mechanisms in the rotary motion that is understood to play the main roles.

Molecular motors manage the different components of the cell as they move within the structures of the cell. By moving along nanoscale tracks a nanoscale molecular motor called kinesis carries molecular cargo through the cell. In reality, it is the smallest train in the world. For the single transduction in the human ear, they are responsible. It was observed by Peter Dallas and his collegians in the northwestern part and this case, it is known as a pristine. Motional energy and acceleration can be provided by molecular motors. Molecular motors which evolve through the march of life are one of the many complex nanostructures.

Neuro-electronic interfaces:-

In the future, the topics which have been discussed so far may be used. Visionary aims of nanotechnology will now be discussed neuro electronic interfaces are included in this. It is the idea of producing more devices that will join the computers and connect them to the system. The building of molecular structure is needed for the production of neuroelectronic interfaces which will allow the detection and control of nerve impulses through an external computer. But the combination of bionanotechnology and computational nanotechnology is the challenge forward; the nerves help in the flow of electric currents between the brain and the nerve center throughout the body and thus are responsible for converging messages in the body. For these signals, the most useful ions are potassium (K) and sodium (Na) and for following a central feel, they move along the channels. Through the nervous system, facial sensations move from the local nerve to the brain which intercepts and processes them. Often a response may be brought by this process which is being filtered into the muscular system. The objective of the nerve electronic interface technique is to allow the registration interpretation. The challenges are the nanostructure that will give an interface that must be compatible with the body's immune system. The muscular system performs certain motions by sensing the ionic currents and causing currents to flow backward obviously, the structure must be molecular conductors whose over-conduction can link with ionic motion in nerve fibers.

Dental durability and cosmetics:-

If we replace the upper enamel layer of teeth with covalently bonded artificial materials like sapphire, they will become more durable and their appurtenance can be improved. These materials are about 20 -100 times hard and strong than natural enamel which is the hardest part of our body, harder than acne bones. As pure diamond and sapphire are proven to fracture and be brittle, they have to be made fracture resistant. This can be done by nanostructure composite material that has embedded carbon nanotubes.

Supra gingival and sub-gingival surfaces can be patrolled by the nanorobotic dentifrice delivered by toothpaste and mouthwash. This will trap the organic matter and alter it into odorless and harmless vapors and ultimately perform continuous calculus debridement. The disease-causing bacteria in the plague can be found 'and then ruined by the properly configured dentil robots. Nanotechnology can exploit molecular or atomic properties of materials and then develop new materials with better properties. The properties of many types of fibers have been improved by nanotechnology. A larger surface area per unit mass is posses by polymer nanofibers if their diameters are in the nanometer range. Easier addition of surface functionalities will be allowed by them as compared to polymer microfibers. For successful dental implants, osteoblast adhesion is important. It is used because of a high degree of nanometer surface roughness.

To produce nanocomposites non agglomerated discrete nanoparticles are manufactured in the coating. The benefit includes high flexible strength superior hardness, translucency, high polish, modulus of elasticity, excellent color, density, polish retention, and excellent handling properties.Dispersible and unique nanoparticles are produced by nano solutions. The operator can be sure about a thing that is perfectly mixed every time as nanotechnology in aversive agents ensures homogeneity. A unique addition of siloxane impression material can be produced by the nanofillers that are integrated into the vinyl siloxanes. Detailed precision can be increased by better flow and improved hydrophilic.

Protein engineering:-

In biological systems, there are the most important molecules called proteins. Body parts that consist of proteins include hair, muscles, fingernails, skin, blood, and eyes. There are many protein-based diseases. Some diseases are caused due to the improper shape of proteins. Such diseases are Cruezfeld-Jacob and mad cow diseases. Genetically inherited diseases are also caused by misfolded or improperly shaped proteins like sickle cell anemia and Tay-Sachs. Protein molecules are made up of long strings of subunits. Proteins consist of twenty natural subunits called amino acids. Hence when a protein molecule is digested, it breaks down into amino acids. Twenty non-natural amino acids and some additional natural amino acids can be stringed together into appropriate long strings so that artificial proteins can be made. These proteins can be used in medicine as well as other applications like synthetic foods. This is the objective of protein engineering. Protein engineering is often known as biotechnology. Originally, biotechnology included the production of particular proteins by using synthetic DNA methods. Protein-producing mechanisms of ordinary organisms like E. Coli have been hijacked. E. Coli is a bacterium that is found in the elementary canal. The proteins can be designed as the genetic code which allows a particular DNA to produce a particular protein is known. Using this method, in medicine, a lot of proteins have been made and even used. The human growth factor is a particularly shrinking case that has been widely used in medicine and also which is produced by nanotechnology. As we know how to make a large number of proteins, one of the more mature areas of nanobiotechnology is protein Engineering. New fields of proteomics and post-genomic science along with the mapping of the human genome have been used to understand the functions of proteins and how their functions can be improved or modified by synthetic structures is also studied.

Chemistry and environment remediation applications:-

Two prominent examples where nanotechnology has played an important role are filtration techniques and chemical catalysis. Synthesis provides or gives novel materials with tailored features and chemical properties. In this way, we can easily accept that chemistry is in reality a basic nanoscience. Energy and time-saving strategies will be provided by a superior process such as self-assembly. In the short run, novel nanomaterials will be provided by chemistry. In terms of nanotechnology, all chemical synthesis can be understood due to the ability to produce certain molecules. Chemistry, which provides polymers, tailor-made molecules, etc., forms a base for nanotechnology.

Catalysis:-

Chemical catalysis benefits from nanoparticles due to their enhanced or high surface area-to-volume ratio. For the production of chemicals, catalysis is significant. The range of nanoparticles in catalysis is from fuel cells to catholic devices. Of the extremely high surface area of nanoparticles, some amount of platinum needed is reduced.

Platinum nanoparticles are regarded in the following generation of automated catalytic converters. Nevertheless, if methane is mingled with the ambient air, the experiments will combust. Many concerns have been raised as the result. Authentic usefulness for catalytic applications may be resolved.

Become an essential application in the future. Possible Toxicity must be investigated with care.

Filtration:-

On air purification, waste-water treatment, and energy storage devices, nanotechnology has a strong effect. For effective filtration techniques, chemical or mechanical methods can be used. For mechanical filtration, nanoporous membranes are considered suitable with pores below 10 nm and membranes should be made of nanotubes. For the separation of different fluids or the removal of ions, nanofiltration is mainly used. The membrane filtration techniques, which work between 10 and 100 nm, are named ultrafiltration. Ultrafiltration technique is also used in renal dialysis.

By using magnetic separation techniques, magnetic nanoparticles remove heavy metal contaminants from wastewater. Compared to the conventional filtration and precipitation method, the use of nanoscale particles is cheap as well as it enhances the efficiency to absorb contaminants. Many water treatment devices are on the market which incorporate nanotechnology. Separation membrane methods are effective in producing potable water cheap nanostructures. Nanotechnology also has a lot of environmental applications. These include providing clean water from wastewater resources. These materials detect and clean up the environment incxpensive detection of impurities and purification of water, nanotechnology can afford to provide clean drinking water.

Along with nanostructures filters, the deionization method has been a device that will reduce the cost and energy needs of removing salts from waste. Nanoparticles can be used to clean industrial waste from groundwater by chemical reactions. The methods which require pumping of water out of the ground for treatment are more costly than this method which is performed at a lower cost. We oven from small wires of potassium manganese oxide, researchers have developed a nanofabricate' paper trowel'. Many nanotechnologies – based filters like air filters, many air-plane cabins, etc. allow mechanical filtration in which nanoscale pores are produced by fiber materials. Nanotechnology is based on filters that are used in almost 80% of the U.S.A.

Harmful biological or chemical agents in the air and soil with very high reactivity can be detected, identified, and filtered by new nanotechnology-enabled sensors and solutions. For separating CO_2 from power plant exhaust, carbon nanotube scrubbers are being investigated by researchers around the world. Particles like self-assembled layers on mesoporous supports, carbon nanotubes, dendrimers, and metal uroporphyrinogen are being investigated to find how to apply unique physical and chemical properties for many types of *toxic site remediation.*

As we know that about 50% of people in India do not have clean drinking water. It is a major issue of concern. A mission has to be started for water detoxification, water purification, and water desalination by using nanosensors and nanomembranes which can identify disease-causing germs and contaminants present in water. A simple method has been devised by the researchers of Banaras Hindu University. This has been done so that contaminants from water and hydrocarbon from petroleum can be removed nano method is used for controlling the cylindrical geometry of those structures which are completely made of carbon nanotubes. The Ministry of human resource development and the department of science and technology in India has supported this.

This will enable the people to get rid of this situation. By spraying benzene into a tube-shaped quartz mold and heating the mold, we can produce the cylinders. Energy independence has been the highest and first priority of our ratio. Filters are made reusable, stronger, and heat resistant by the nanotube compositions. A level of precision suitable for varied uses is offered by carbon nanotubes. They can remove 25 nm polioviruses and larger pathogens such as E. coli from water. It is believed by the researchers that filters can be made adaptable to microfluid uses which are involved in removing or separating chemicals in drug discovery. In nanoscience, this is the latest classic application. Water born diseases such as cholera etc. will be minimized the water will be made safe and clean.

Energy applications:-

Concerned with energy, the most advanced nanotechnology projects include storage, conversion, production improvements by decreasing materials and process rates, energy savings, and arise renewable energy sources. For developing affordable clean and renewable energy sources, many researchers one looking for different ways along with the means to reduce toxicity burdens on the environment. Promising cheap solar power in the future, solar panels are more capable is change solar energy into electrical energy.

They are inexpensive to manufacture and easier to install. It has been suggested by new research that future solar converters might be paintable. The demand from the sector will increase from 120,000 MW to 4,00,000 MWW when our population will reach 1.4 billion. Four basic energy sources are accessed by electric power including feasible fuels like coal natural gas and oil. It is fortunate for up that 88% of the energy used for power generation is indigenous of which 55% of energy is used from coal, 25% of the energy used from hydroelectricity, 3% of energy from nuclear power, and 5% of energy is used from renewable energy sources. Only 2% of energy is contributed by the solar energy segment. On natural gas and oil, 11% of the energy used for electric power generation is independent but they are mostly imported at enormous costs. Only 1% of oil is used every year for producing electricity. Nevertheless, on high-cost gas supplies, 10% of power generation is independent. 20 to 25 % of energy may be targeted by the power produced by renewable energy technologies, against the present 5%.

For the use of nanotechnology in partnership with Penn state university innovative solution can be found using higher efficiency carbon nanotube that is based on solar photo voltaic cells with an efficiency of 45%. Modular 100 MW solar SPV plants can be set up across the country as a result and in reduced land with a cost of about Rs. twenty crores per MW SPV plant with 14% efficiency on photovoltaic storage based on carbon nanotube for storage of energy.

- *By better catalysis nanotechnology can improve the efficiency of fuel production from normal and low-grade raw petroleum materials, vehicles and power plants can be made more efficient by reducing friction and high-energy combustion fuel.*
- *The aim of nano-bioengineering of enzymes is the convert cellulose into ethanol from corn stalks, wood chips, unfertilized perennial grasses, etc.*
- *Less flammable, rapid charging lightweight, and well-efficient batteries use nanotechnology. The common and nontoxic virus is used in a new lithium-ion battery.*
- *For alternative transportation techniques at a decreased cost, nanostructure materials make better hydrogen membranes and catalysts and storage materials needed to realize fuel tanks. A safe and lightweight hydrogen fuel tank is being developed by researchers. Longer, stronger, and lightweight blades of windmills are made of epoxy-containing carbon nanotubes. This will increase the amount of electricity generated.*
- *To have low resistance than high-tension wires, researchers are developing wires containing carbon nanotubes. This will decrease the transmission power loss.*
- *Thin film solar electric panels are being developed by researchers to power mobile electronic devices. To generate useful energy from friction lighter body temperature, these panels can be fitted on computer cases and flexible piezoelectric nanowires woven into clothing.*

- *Products known as energy efficiency products have experienced an increase in the number and types of applications. Additionally, more efficient lighting systems are included in these for vastly decreased energy use for stronger and lighter vehicle chassis materials for the transportation field.*

Reduction of energy consumption:-

Energy consumption can be decreased by the use of more efficient lighting or combustion systems and by utilizing stronger and lighter materials in the transportation sector. Currently, light bulbs change only 5% of electrical energy into light energy. Nanotechnological approaches like light-emitting diodes (LED) or quantum-caged atoms (QCAS) can decrease energy consumption for illumination.

Increasing the efficiency of energy production:-

Nanotechnology used nanostructure can increase the efficiency of light conversion with a continuum of band gaps. The internal combustion engine has an efficiency of 30 to 40% of the movement. Nanotechnology can improve combustion by designing specific catalysis with maximized surface area. A spray was developed on nanoparticle substances by scientists at Toronto University in 2005. When this substance is applied to the surface, it can instantly transform itself into a solar collector.

The use of more eco-friendly energy systems:-

The use of fossil fuels powered by hydrogen is an example of an environmentally friendly form of energy. Probably the most prominent nanostructured materials are the catalysis which is made of carbon and supported model metal particles having diameters between 1-5 nm. Zeolites, nanotubes, or atlantes that are nanostructured materials are being investigated. Small nanosized pores are present in the materials which can store hydrogen. Combustion engine pollutants can be reduced by nanoporous filters that will clean the exhaust by catalytic converters.

Recycling of batteries:-

Operating time is limited and replacement or recharging is required due to the energy densities of batteries. The disposal system is represented by a large number of spent batteries and accumulators. The problem of the battery disposal systems can be solved by using rechargeable batteries or supercapacitors with a higher rate of recharging using nanomaterials.

Information and communication applications:-

On conventional top-down strategies, high-technique production processes are based. Integrated circuits have a critical length scale at the nanoscale at 50 nm or below in comparison to the gate length of transistors in CPU and DRAM devices. To provide smaller, faster, and more portable systems, nanotechnology is used in computing communications and other electronics applications. These systems can manage other electronic applications. These systems can manage and store large amounts of information. These applications involve:

- *By using nanoscale transistors computers' memory can be stored in only one chip. These transistors are fast, more powerful, and energy efficient.*
- *During a system shutdown enabled by nanometer-scale magnetic tunnel junctions, encrypted data can be saved by magnetic random access memory. Thus play features can be resumed and vehicle accident data can be collected.*
- *Organic light-emitting diodes (OLED) are nanostructured polymer films. Organic light-emitting diodes are in corporate displays for many new TV, phones, computers, digital cameras, laptops, cell phones, and other devices. OLED screens provide images wider. Viewing angles, better picture density, lower power consumption, lighter weight, and longer lifetimes.*
- *Flash memory chips for iPods, antibacterial or anti microbial coatings on keyboards, mouse cell phone casings, ultra-responsive hearing aids, and flexible displays for e-book readers are included in computing and electronic products.*

Memory storage:-

In the past, electronic memory designs depended on the formation of transistors. Researchers have been offered an alternative to crossbar switch-based electronics to produce ultra-high-density memories. Two leaders developed NANO-RAM and Hewlett Packard which is a carbon nanotube-based crossbar memory.

Novel semiconductor devices:-

For nanosized objects, this effect can be significantly amplified. The data storage density of hard disks has been increased by the GMR effect which stands for Giant Magneto resistance. This has made the gigabyte range possible. The tunneling magnetic (TMR) is based on the spin-independent tunneling of electrons by the adjacent ferromagnetic layers. Both GMR and TMR effects can create nonvolatile main memory for computers such as magnetic random access memory (MRAM). In 1999 CMOS transistors tested the limits of the principles of MOSFET transition.

Laboratories for electronic and information technology were performed in this way in France. CMOS transistors were not only a simple research experiment. Rather it was a demonstration work to study how CMOS technology functions. At present, it is possible to master the coordinated assembly of a large no. of these transistors. Also, it is not possible to develop this on an industrial level.

Novel optoelectronic devices:-

Optoelectronic devices are replacing conventional analog electrical devices because of their very large capacity and bandwidth. Two promising examples include quantum dots and photonic crystals. A lattice that is half of the wavelengths of light used is contained in photonic crystals. For the propagation of different wavelengths, they resemble a semiconductor for light or photons. Quantum dots, used for the construction of lasers, are nanoscale objects. The wavelength emitted by the quantum dots depends on the diameter of the dot. This is their advantage over election semiconductor lasers. Also as compared to traditional lasers, these are cheaper as well as offer a higher beam quality.

Displays:-

Using carbon nanotubes displays can be produced with low energy consumption. With very high efficiency for field emission displays (FED), carbon nanotubes can be used as field emitters because they have a small diameter of a few nanometers and are electrically conductive. Cathode ray tube resembles the principle of operation.

Quantum computers:-

Quantum mechanics are explained by new approaches in computing for novel quantum computers. Rapid quantum algorithms will be used as a result. For many computations, quantum computers have a quantum bit memory space that is termed a cubit. In this way, we can improve the performance of older systems.

ICT:-

The next generations of computers will be improved by molecular switches and circuits with the nanoscale. Low cost, low power, nano size, and rapid assemblies will be achieved by ultra-dense computer memory. As a result, tiny measurements assembly of computers, tablet PCs, laptops, etc. will come into existence. New devices having uses in electronics, structure, health care and satellite systems have been introduced with the emergence of nanotechnology. It is only due to the collaboration and cooperation among researchers in electronics, materials and computer science, physics, chemistry and biology, and electrical engineering that progress in nanotechnology is spurred. This emerging area has brought development and research by combining the strengths of multiple domain knowledge and synergy.

Future transportation applications:-

Many means to improve the transportation infrastructure are offered by nanotechnology. There are as follows:

- *Nanoscale devices and sensors have provided cost-effective continuous structural monitoring of the condition and performance of tumors, bridges, parking structures, rails, and payment sensors.*
- *Increased transport infrastructures can also be supported by them. For maintaining lane position, avoiding collisions, and adjusting travel routes, this infrastructure can communicate with vehicle-based systems. This is to circumnavigate congestion and other such activities.*
- *Innovative capability can be incorporated into conventional infrastructure materials by the new systems. For instance, the ability to generate or transmit energy. By future sensor systems, multiple physical phenomena can be used for sensing a variety of analytics for many applications. Light is measured by the optical transducer, electrical properties are measured by the chemical transducer, and transition to the local magnetic field is measured by a mechanical transducer.*

To aircraft manufacturing, stronger and lighter materials will be of immense use. Nanotechnology has its effects on spacecraft where weight is the major factor. The size of equipment would be decreased by nanotechnology and as a result, the fuel consumption needed to get it airborne will also decrease. By using nanotech materials weight of hang gliders can be halved and their toughness and strength can be increased. The mass of supercapacitors can be lowered by nanotech materials. To give power to the assistive electrical motors these supercapacitors will be used so that hang gliders off flatland can be launched.

Emerging technologies such as Nano, MEMS, Information technology, space research, biotechnology, hypersonic, microwave, high-power lasers, etc. will dominate the energy field shortly. A major thrust will be given to the realization of advanced aerospace systems through advances in materials science and technology. Bio, nano, and information technologies will prove to be very helpful in the coming generation, of aerospace, and products. For future aerospace systems, molecular nanotechnology has a lot of abilities. Research has illustrated that high-temperature materials may be made by carbon nanotubes and they can survive even in a vacuum and other harsh environments. Carbon nanotubes, with remarkable mechanical and electrical properties, are the normal form of carbon. It has been hoped that these kinds of materials can revolutionize electronic design. In the field of material science, carbon nanotubes will result in composites that are lightweight, super strong, tiny, and intelligent structures. This has a lot of aerospace applications.

Construction:-

Construction is made cheaper, faster, safer, and more varied by nanotechnology. From advanced homes to massive skyscrapers structures can be created even more rapidly and at a much lower rate.

Refineries:-

Impurities can be removed by refineries from the materials like aluminum or steel etc. by using nanotech materials.

Vehicle manufacturers:-

Lighter, stronger, faster, and safer products will be useful for producing vehicles. Heat-resistant and more hare-wearing parts should be used to construct combustion engines.

Consumer Goods:-

Many consumer products can be provided by nanotechnology which ranges from scratch resistant to easy-to-clean. This can make life easier and pleasanter. Stain resistance and wrinkle replant modern textiles are in use nowadays. Clothes will become smarter in the future through wearable electronics embedded in them. Different types of nanoparticles are already in use. Especially in the field of cosmetics, such kind of novel products has promising potential.

Foods:-

Nanotechnology has the potential to solve scientific and engineering challenges in food. The bioprocessing industry can manufacture safe and high-quality food through sustainable and efficient means. Nanoencapsulation of bioactive food compounds; intelligent, smart, and active food packaging systems, etc. are involved in the energy applications of nanotech for the food industry. Food can be produced processed and packed using nanotechnology. Food packaging can be improved by placing anti-microbial agents directly on the surface of the coated film. Nanocomposites can reduce or enhance gas permeability. For different products, the gas permeability of different fillers is required.

Nano-foods:-

At the rate of 3 to 4 per week, nanotech produces consumer products that are coming into the market. On PEN's list, three foods are present. These include Canola Active oil, a brand of canola cooking oil; nano team, nanocavities slim shake chocolate. nanodrop is an additive that is present in canola oil. This is by information posted on PEN's website. These drops are designed to carry vitamins, minerals, and phytochemicals. Infused nanoclusters are used in the shake according to U.S manufacturer RBC life sciences Inc. cocoa to increase the health and taste benefits of cocoa without the presence of any extra sugar.

Household:-

In households, the most prominent and useful app; the actions of nanotechnology involve self-cleaning and easy-to-clean surfaces on glass. Nano ceramic particles can improve heat resistance and smoothness of common household equipment like iron etc.

Optics:-

The first sunglasses on the market which use anti-reflective and protective ultrathin polymer coatings. Scratch-resistant surface coatings based on nanocomposite are offered by nanotechnology. Nano-optics could allow for an increase.

Textiles:-

Engineered nanofibers can make clothes water and stain-repellent or wrinkle-free. With a nanotechnological finish, textiles can be washed at lower temperatures and less frequently. Tiny carbon particles membrane can be integrated by nanotechnology. It provides a guarantee for full surface protection to the wearer from electrostatic charges. Several other applications like Textiles Nanotechnology Laboratory at Cornell University have been developed by research institutes.

Cosmetics:-

Nanotechnology has many applications in sunscreen. Ultraviolet production which is traditional suffers from poor long-term stability. Based on mineral nanoparticles sunscreen provides many advantages like titanium dioxide. As the particle size is reduced, titanium dioxide loses the cosmetically undesirable whitening. Titanium dioxide nanoparticles have a UV protection property.

Agriculture:

Nanotechnology can change the agriculture sector and food industry. Nanotechnology creates different changes in this sector from packaging, processing, and production to conservation, transportation, and waste treatment. The production cycle can be redesigned, conservation and processing processes can be restructured and the food habits of the people can be redefined by Nanoscience concepts and nanotechnology applications.

Low production in cultivable areas, shrinking of cultivable areas, wastage of inputs such as particles, fertilizers, water, food insecurity, etc. are the main areas in agriculture or farming in which nanotechnology has failed. These are the main challenges to nanotechnology. With reduced land, water, and workforce, we are on the mission of generating 400 tons of food grams. To bring employment in rural areas it is significant to take agro-processing in a big way. In food processing and agriculture, some possible areas include nanoporous zeolites for slow release and efficient doses of water and fertilizers for plants. These areas are also involved in nanocapsules for herbicide delivery, nanosensors for soil quality, and plant health monitoring. Nanocomposites for plastic film coatings are researched and are used in food packaging, and antimicrobial nanoemulsions for uses in the decontamination of food equipment packaging, or food processing.

CHAPTER VI

IMPACTS OF NANOTECHNOLOGY

Introduction:-

Water purification systems, physical enhancement, energy systems, improved manufacturing methods, nanomedicine and nutrition and infrastructure, fabrication, etc are involved in the major benefits of nanotechnology. They may decrease labor, maintenance requirements, and land.

Potential risks involve safety, health environmental issues, transitional effects like displacement of conventional industries, military uses like implants for soldiers, and biological welfare. If the potential impacts of nanoparticles are ignored these can be significant potential risks of nanoparticles being dealt with by regulatory bodies like the United States environmental protection agency. The organic food sector was produced in Australia and the UK, and recently in Canada, along with all food certified to Demeter International standards.

Health and Safety Impact of Nanotechnology:-

The presence of nanoparticles is a certain aspect that makes them risky, mostly in their increased reactivity and mobility. Certain properties of nanoparticles can be faced with real hazards if they are hazardous to the environment or human beings. It can be called nano pollution in this case.

Two kinds of nanostructures need to be differentiated in addressing the environmental and health effects of nanoparticles. These nanostructures are

1. Nanostructures surface nano components and nanocomposites. In these, the incorporation of nano-scale particles into a material device or substance takes place.

2. Free nanoparticles where individual nanoparticles of a substance are present.

Tease-free nanoparticles could be simple compounds where nanoparticles of a particular element are coated with other substances. The immediate concern is with nanoparticles although awareness of materials containing fixed nanoparticles is also important. Adverse impacts of nanoparticles can't be derived from the known toxicity of macro-sized materials as they are very different from their everyday counterparts. Significantly, a liquid or powder having nanoparticles should contain a range of particle sizes. It must not be monodisperse. A tendency to aggregate is shown by nanoparticles. Sometimes from individual nanoparticles behavior of such aggregates is different. The initial research on how workers might be exposed to nano-sized particles in the industrial use of nanomaterials and how nanoparticles interact with the body's system has been conducted by the National institute for occupational safety and health. Interim guidelines for working with nanomaterials have been offered by NIOSH.

To study the impact of nanoparticles on NIOSH-certified and EU-marked respirators, a study has been conducted at the National Personal Protective Technology Laboratory of NISOH is regarded with the filter penetration of nanoparticles. It has been found that leak size was the largest factor in the number of nanoparticles found inside the respirators of test dummies. The most particle size range was between near about 30-100 nanometers. It has been proposed by E. Marla Filcher that the consumer product safety commission is ill-occupied to oversee the safety of complex and high-tech products.

This commission is charged with saving people from unreasonable hazards of death or injury concerned with consumer products. The impacts of nanotechnology are not politicized or characterized by society.

Health impacts:-

The potential health hazards posed by exposure to nanotechnology and the potential for nanotechnological in nations to have medical uses to treat diseases' potential health risks of nanomaterials are studied in the field of nanotoxicology. The human body readily takes up small-sized nanotechnology materials rather than large-sized particles. One of the important issues that need to be resolved is how the nanoparticles behave inside the organism. It is not known what occurs if slowly degradable or non-degradable nanoparticles get collected in the human body organs. This is due to their large surface. It is hard to generalize about health risks concerned with exposure to nanoparticles as the large no. of variables affecting toxicity. In the companies, busy creating nanomaterials and labs engaged in nanotechnological research, health and environmental issues combine. The medical application of nanotechnology is nanomedicine. Nanomedicine has been used or utilized in nanoelectronic biosensors.

It can also be applied to the upcoming applications of molecular nanotechnology. It has been presumed that a set of clinically useful and helpful devices and research tools may be preceded by nanomedicine in the coming time. New commercial uses in the pharmaceutical industry are expected by the national name technology initiative. These uses or applications include new drug delivery systems, new therapies, and in vivo imaging. Nanoelectronics-based sensors and neuro electronics interfaces are the other active goals of the research. Cell repair machines can revolutionize medical and medical science. It is believed by the speculative field of molecular nanotechnology.

Food security:-

The probability of monitoring disease-causing germs on crops and line stock along with measurement of crop productivity is offered by tiny sensors. Additionally, the efficiency of fertilizers can be enhanced by nanoparticles. Nevertheless, according to a report given in 2004 by the Swiss Rewarned company, the ability to potentially toxic substances can be enhanced to penetrate deep layers of soil and travel over long distances. Additionally, researchers in both developing and developed are attempting or trying very hard they can make those crops that can grow in unfriendly conditions like in soil having a low level of water or in soil containing high amounts of salts. They are trying to achieve this by manipulating the crop's genetic materials on a nanotechnological scale with biological molecules.

Environmental impacts:-

The opposition has been spray painted on a former fort less above the city by the groups opposing the installation of nanotechnological laboratories in Grenoble France. A genetic name for all waste produced by nanodevices is nano pollution. This waste is produced during the nanomaterials manufacturing process. This type of waste can penetrate easily into plant and animal cells causing hazardous effects. It can even float in the air. Thus, it is considered or regarded as very dangerous. A living organism may not have the correct methods to deal with nano waste as nanoparticles do not appear in nature and are made by humans. The complete life cycle of these particles needs to be evaluated to access the health risks of engineered nanoparticles. Nanoparticles present new environmental effects so environmental assessment is justified. Concerns about nano-pollution are being raised by scrims along with the discussion or argument that it is at present impossible to assume or control the ecological effect of the release of these nano-products into the environment.

Besides, the environment can obtain benefits from the future applications of nanotechnology. Ions can be removed and different fluids can be separated by mechanical filtration for which membranes with very small pores of less than 10 nm are suitable. Afterward, for removing heavy metal contaminants from wastewater, magnetic nanoparticles are used which will provide a reliable and effective method.

As compared to conventional filtration and precipitation methods, the use of nanoparticles is cheap and it also enhances the efficiency to absorb contaminants from wastewater. Researchers are trying their best to use nanomaterials for different purposes involving more efficient solar cells, practical fuel cells, and eco-friendly batteries. Thus it can be concluded from observations that nanotechnology has an important role to play in clean energy production.

Regulation Impact:-

This discussion is concerned with the conditions for which it is essential and appropriate to achieve new materials before releasing them in the market environment and community. Regulatory bodies such as the United States Environment Protection Agency and the food and drug administration in the U.S., health and consumer protection directorate of the European Commission risks posed by nanoparticles. Bulk and nanoscale sizes of materials are sometimes not differentiated by the material safety data sheet that needs to be issued for some materials. Even if they are distinguished, these MEOS are advisory only. Human and environmental health and safety impacts related to nanotechnology may be exacerbated by limited nanotechnology labeling and regulation. It will be important to make sure that potential risks don't over have the potential advantage of nanotechnology.

These risks are concerned with the research and commercial application of nanotechnology. To meet community expectations of nanotechnology and ensure the indulgence of public interests in shaping the development of nanotechnology regulation may be needed.

Societal impacts:-

Across many different sectors, nanotechnology has a large number and variety of applications nanotechnology poses broader social challenges. Social issues of nanotechnology should be assessed. Social scientists have proposed that. Development in technology should be in such a way that it meets social objectives. The challenges should be factored into upstream decision making and research public participation should be included in governance and technology assessment. This has been suggested by many social organizations and scientists in civil society. On the instrumental level, the societal risks from the use of nanotechnology involve the probability of military applications of nanotechnology along with increased surveillance capabilities by nanosensors.

To clean patents at the nanoscale, the previous few years have witnessed a gold rush. In 2003, over 800 nano-related patents were granted. This no is enhancing year to year to year. On nanoscale inventions and discoveries, corporations are taking out broad-ranging patents. For instance, two corporations that hold basic patents on carbon nanotubes are NEC and IBM. Carbon nanotubes are the present cornerstones of nanotechnology. Carbon nanotubes are becoming very important in several industries. They are used in computers and electronics to strengthen materials for drug delivery and diagnostics. Nevertheless, with their expanding use for selling carbon nanotubes, one must buy a license from IBM or NEC. Nanotechnology can have a beneficial effect on the vast majority of people all around the world. It can make resources more efficient unit and sustainable. Nevertheless, it has also potential negative effects on society like privacy, social divide, communications, and risk.

Privacy:-

Useful information like pollution levels and traffic conditions etc. can be given by ambient sensor systems. Information about individual activities can also be transmitted by them. Generally, through the legislative system, the limits on the kind of information that can be collated or captured need to be clearly defined by society. Privacy issues may allow doctors to routinely screen people for the presence of genetic diseases. They arise through advances in medical diagnostics. If this technique is made compulsory to allow earlier treatment then what about the patient's right to choose? If not then will health insurance companies demand it as a prerequisite?

Social divide:-

Nanotechnology can create divisions between rich and poor or developed and developing countries. As we know the benefit of advances in transport, health care, energy supplies, etc. will be taken mostly by the wealthy as the poor can't afford these services. As we know nanomaterials will replace previous minerals and metals that are mined in the developing world. This will decrease our dependency on our revealed resources. The development ad economy of these countries will be threatened due to this and loss of this and loss of this revenue will harm them. Nanotechnology strategies, that address country's needs, are being exploited in many countries to address these potential impacts.

Communications:-

It is only due to the communications and discussions between scientists, and the government's wider social and industrialists that new developments and wide-ranging impacts of nanotechnology can be accepted. Risks and advantages concerned with the new development have been misinformed and misunderstood due to the ignorance of this in the past. Many research funding agencies, governments, etc. have recognized this. Many people now are initiatives that find dialogue with interested citizens and social scientists. This will help to explain the implications of new developments.

Potential benefits and risks for developing countries:-

In developing countries, many people don't have attention to basic services like safe water, health care, reliable energy, and education. New solutions can be provided to these problems of people through nanotechnology. Millennium development goals have been noted in 2004 by the US task force on science and technology. Science and technology also contain innovations involving production using small labor, maintenance, low price, more productivity, and needs for energy and materials.

Scientists are researching some other nanotechnologies such as water purification systems, food production, energy system and medicine, pharmaceuticals, and information and communication. On the other hand, some fields of nanotechnology are quite far away from development. Many factors affect human health and the environment in developing countries. Many factors involve the lack of readiest environmental, worker safety, and human health regulations. Unenforced or poorly enforced regulation, also responsible for this cause is connected to a lack of human and physical capacity. Sometimes for developing the institutional and scientific capacity for assessing and managing risks, some nations need to be provided especially financial help.

They may also require essential infrastructure like laboratories and techniques for detection. Nevertheless, there are concerns that only efficient nations will get the advantages concerned with nanotechnology. Most of the research and development associated with nanotechnology is carried out in developed countries like the USA, Japan, France, Canada, etc. Additionally, some new multinational techniques such as IBM, Micron technologies, Intel, advanced micro devices, etc. have the concentration of most patents related to nanotechnology. Now, it has created a fear among developing countries that they won't have the infrastructure required for nanotechnology research.

Many farmers, live hoods depend on natural products like rubber, coffee, and tea. The economy of developing countries, which depends on these export crops, will be livelily influenced by their substitution with industrial nano products.

Impacts of molecular nanotechnology:-

A different scenario known as green goo has been forwarded with the advent of nano biotech. Here, the malignant substance is a self-replicating organism engineered by nanotechnology rather than nanobots. The cheap creation of unbelievably powerful products and devices is achieved by molecular manufacturing. Damage caused is really large like low-flying supersonic aircraft injuring or harming many animals and the collection of solar energy on a large scale for modifying the planet's albedo will directly influence the environment.

Much larger machines able to excavate or destroy large areas of the planet can be stronger materials. This problem is a major cause of worry if large no. of activity and purpose damaging the environment is taken to extremes. An aggregate of individual actions may result in such forms of damage which are harmful.

CHAPTER VII

ADVANTAGES AND DISADVANTAGES OF NANOTECHNOLOGY

Introduction:-

At its basic level, nanotechnology is based on the principles of controlling matter. His technique is about the controlling of matter at a molecular or atomic level. Nanotechnology has been successful in various fields such as medicine and electronics. In the production of new materials, nanotechnology is proving to be helpful. But as we know that everything has positive and negative sides so along with advantages nanotechnology has many disadvantages. It may pose threat to the life forms on earth.

- ***Now, we will discuss the advantages and disadvantages of nanotechnology***

  Advantages of nanotechnology:-

- *For the prevention of graying issues and hair loss, nanotechnology is greatly used.*
- *Aged women who want to look gorgeous and elegant use wrinkle-free creams which have been brought by the cosmetic range from L'Oreal. As these products involve the nanoscience of pro-retinol A, they have given immediate results.*
- *Nanoparticles are useful in the repair of skin tissues due to their extremely small size which can easily penetrate the skin. Only due to this, we can prevent skin aging by using nanotech products.*
- *Sunscreens used by millions contain nanoparticles like titanium dioxide and zinc oxide.*
- *A lot of electronic products, applications, and procedures can be revolutionized by name technology. Name transistors, plasma displays, nano diodes, quantum computers, OLED, etc. are the areas that have benefitted a lot from nanotechnology.*
- *The manufacturing sector is another industry that benefits from nanotechnology this sector requires nanotubes nanoparticles, aerogels, and*

other similar items for producing their products. The materials which are not produced by nanotechnology are heavier, less durable, and fragile as compared to nanotech products.

- *The energy sector is also benefited from nanotechnology. More efficient devices can be produced through this technology through the development of more effective energy absorbing energy producing and energy storage products are smaller. There are many such types of items such as fuel cells, batteries, and solar cells which can be built smaller and more effectively using this technology.*
- *Nanotechnology has also proved itself in the medical field. It can help in creating smart drugs that will make treatment faster. These don't have any side effects as conventional drugs have. Research is underway for using nanotechnology in bone repair, tissue regeneration, immunity, and care for life-threatening diseases like cancer, diabetes, etc. thus, nanotechnology is a boon for medicine.*
- *The tiniest size of transistors on silicon microscopic near zero is about to reach its limit in the information technology industry. It has been assumed by Moore's law that we must be working at an atomic level by 2015. The new generation of smaller more powerful components will be developed by nanotechnology. The development of a memory device that can store all the information in the United State national library and has the size as that of a sugar cube is the goal of the U.S. government's nanotechnology initiative.*
- *PCs will be able to operate on one tiny battery for decades and will have the size as that of a grain of the land. Computers will be made invisible due to nanotechnology. Materials will incorporate computation as they will be engineered on the molecular scale. The physical process in the human brain will be reverse-engineered by scientists in the next 25 years. This will result in biologically inspired computers.*
- *With nanotechnology, glasses will display images directly into our retimes, virtual reality will become much more life-like and contact lenses will allow fuel immersion in virtual reality.*
- *The ozone layer can be rebuilt atom by atom through eco-friendly airborne nanorobots oil spillages could to removed completely and quickly. Water sources can be purified which will save the lives of millions of people. In the future, pollution will only be a thing in the dream as pollutants will be reduced to their component atoms and can be recycled. Nanotechnology will eliminate the dependence on the earth's natural resources for our energy.*

- *Advanced speech recognition will be utilized by nanotechnology for the earning impaired. This will create subtitles automatically and on the fly. Reading machines for blind people will be corporate into clothing and use advanced text recognition which will enable the users to read minus, signs, displays, etc. Text information can be translated from one language to another by using similar nanotechnology devices.*

Disadvantages of nanotechnology:-

- *The loss of jobs in the conventional manufacturing and farming industry is due to the development of nanotechnology.*
- *As alternative sources of energy develop, the value of diamonds and oil fell. This results in the crashing of creation markets. As diamonds will be mass produces, their value will be lost.*
- *It has been found by research that some types of carbon nanotubes can cause mesothelioma and can prove to be very harmful and dangerous.*
- *Due to the very small size of these particles, they can be inhaled and cause problems that a person gets from inhaling small as best particles.*
- *Silver nanoparticles limit the growth of bacteria, they are bacteriostatic. Bacteria assist in breaking organic matter in water treatment plants but this may result in their destruction. Both environmental and medical nanoparticles are harmful. Particles can be made very catalytic due to the high surface area-to-volume ratio.*
- *Nature presents many nanoparticles to which the organisms on earth may have evolved immunity. Nano-regime is made left by the free nanoparticles in the environment that tend to agglomerate quickly. These may of the living organism through cell membranes and interact with biological systems. The result of this interaction is still unknown.*
- *Nanoparticles can be absorbed by macromolecules in an animal body to their large surface.*
- *Certain waste products are released during the manufacturing of nanomaterials. This waste can float in and enter planet or animal cells.*
- *Natural substances may be replaced by nanotechnological products which may pose certain social implications due to their social and environmental implications. The difficulty is for the factory workers and farmers whose level hood relies on the distribution and production of these natural substances. If nanomaterials produced in developed countries start, substituting for their agricultural products then agricultural countries like India will have to face*

financial processes.

- *Nanomaterials contained in sunscreens and cosmetics provide health risks to people all over the world but this fact or reality is not known by many. In a mouse model, the cardiovascular system can be damaged by diesel nanoparticles. They can interfere with the functioning of nature by hindering and obstructing many biological processes.*
- *Nanotechnology has the potential for mask poisoning. This is one of the major disadvantages of nanotechnology. All types of improved new products can be created through nanoscience. But there is one hindrance. The particles produced are so tiny that they may be responsible for causing health risks to the consumers using them.*
- *The products at use nanotechnology are more costly than others. Currently, the cost of developing and manufacturing nanotechnology is very high which is affordable for many. Thus, it is benefits are available only to the richer section of society. Others are deprived of its advantages or benefits.*
- *Researchers will need a second thought to apply nanotechnology in various spheres of life due to its social and environmental implications.*
- *Potential direction nanotechnology is an ethical problem. This can create problems with the possible effects of the products formed.*
- *Many things are included in the practical problems of nanotechnology. These need to be addressed.*

CHAPTER VIII

SCOPE FOR FUTURE

Nanotechnology has the ability to transform society more than the industrial revolution. This will be developed for everyone and will affect or influence everyone. With an extremely right future, nanotechnology is developing rapidly. As compared to the counterpart's products, the uses of nanotechnology are impressive. Speculating about the future of nanotechnology is therefore may be interesting. Engineering of functional systems at a nanoscale or molecular scale is the definition of nanotechnology at the basic level. Through various industrial sectors, nanotechnology has spread widely in almost all major fields. Some applications of nanotechnology can be divided into four generations according to Michael Rocco of the U.S. National nanotechnology. The first generation of nanotechnology started in 2000 as said by Rocco. The first generation designed to perform one task like aerosols and colloids are known as passive nanostructures. Second-generation products are called active nanostructures. This started in 2005. Instances of second-generation products include sensors and actuators.

They have a multitasking ability. In 2010 third generation of nanotechnology began which is the ea of systems of nanosystems. A large no. of interacting objects such as 3D networking and new hierarchical architectures, guided assembling and robotics together for nanosystems. In 2015 when the first integrated nanosystems will be developed, the fourth generation of nanotechnology will start. The things which look impossible today or at present which can't be imagined will be possible in the coming time with the advancement of nanotechnology. With the advancement of nanotechnology, developments in the field of nanotechnology will become propelled. Major problems like contamination of particles and poor dissipation of heat will be solved with the benefits of ultra-high purity materials and innovative technologies. Therefore using these techniques, we can create smaller computer chips with higher speeds. Using hard nanomaterials, capacitors with surprising captaincies values are being produced. There will be more easiness and convenience in the production of miniaturized electronic products.

Extremely fast computers, tiny mobile devices, and other miniaturized electronic devices can be bought in the future with the benefit of these developments. Nanotubes and nanowires have been proven successful in their respective fields. Carbon nanotubes have 50 times higher tensile strength than carbon steels. Using nanotechnology even stronger materials can be produced. As the world is lacking in natural resources such as petroleum and coal, high energy density batteries are given special and prime importance. These batteries can be produced from nanocrystalline materials synthesized by sol-gel technology. These batteries can hold more energy than traditional materials.

One of the major concerns related to the future of nanoscience is molecular manufacturing. From the simple molecular reconstruction of daily use objects, this process can bring the materials to life. The poor nations, that are suffering from a lack of food throughout the year, will get given a prize if this will be made a reality in the future and satisfy the hunger of the world. Nanotechnology has been proven a boon in the medical field. Due to this, injury and illness can be cured at the nanoscale. People won't have to bear the pains of diabetes, cancer, and other life-threatening diseases. With the use of nanosurgery, anything can be identified and repaired in the human body. Not only works that humans can do these will be done by nanorobots. Rather, they could achieve those things which are impossible for humans. Leaving an extremely clean environment, they will clean water and air perfectly at the nano level. They will reduce the cost for humans by being employed in high-tech positions.

After 20 years, it will be difficult to predict the future development in the field of nanotechnology. This has provided a great contribution to shaping the way the world is going. But to face the wonders of nanotechnology, we have to be prepared right now. Nanotechnology is developing and maturing rapidly at present. Between 1997 and 2005, total investment in nanotech development was from $432 million to about $4.1 billion. On the other hand, the corresponding industry investment exceeded that of governments by 2005. Approximately one trillion will be contributed to the global economy by the products in corporation nanotech by 2015. Around two million workers will be employed in nanotech industries and three times this number will get supporting jobs. The description of nanotech fully characterizes it in terms of the small size of its physical features. Though nanotech is nearly looking to use infinitely smaller parts than traditional engineering, that depiction makes it sound.

To control the behavior and properties of matter fundamentally, nanotechnology is viewed as the application of quantum theory and other nanotechnology-specific phenomena. Through overlapping stages of industrial prototyping and early commercialization, nanotechnology will involve in ever next couple of decades. The first stage includes the development of passive infrastructure which began after 2000. The materials with steady structures and functions can be modest as the particles of zinc oxide in sunscreens. In 2005, the second stage began that focused on active nanostructures which can alter their size, conductivity, shape, and other properties during use. Therapeutic molecules can be released in the body by new drug-delivery particles. Electronic components like being decreased to single and complex molecules.

Around 2010, the third stage began. Along with the systems of nanostructures, the workers will cultivate expertise. Guided self-assembly of nanoelectronic components can be included in one application into three-dimensional circuits and whole devices. For improving the tissue compatibility of implants or for creating scaffolds for tissue generation or building artificial organs, medicine could employ such systems. The field of molecular nanosystems heterogeneous networks can be expanded after 2015-2020. In these networks, the molecules and supra-molecular structures will serve as distinct devices. These molecular nanosystems will be enabled to operate much faster in a far wider range of environments. Biological systems are based on water and show sensitivity toward temperatures. On the other hand, proteins inside the cells work collectively in this way.

Robots and computers can be decreased to extraordinary tiny sizes. The ambitiousness of medical applications is similar to those of aging treatments and genetic therapies. Telecommunications can be altered by new interfaces linking people directly to electronics. Nanotechnology has made exponential progress and has built its place among the fastest-growing areas of science and technology. Some of the recent breakthroughs have involved:-

- *They have included the first integrated circuits which utilize 3-D carbon nanotubes. In maintaining the growth of computer power, these could be vital and allow the continuity of Moore's law.*
- *Having 15 nm width filters they involve water purification bottles. This will help the military personnel and civilians to produce safe and clean drinking water.*
- *By using nanomaterials composites military equipment can be made stronger and lighter.*
- *With the use of nanotechnology materials, solar panels are made efficiently and are involved in these breaks through.*
- *Bacteria-resistant, dirt-resistant, and scratch-resistant nanotechnology surfaces.*

- *Recent breakthroughs also involve new fabrics causing the liquid to fall off without learning any dampness or stains. It states that they are hilly and resistant to liquid.*
- *Nanostructured polymers are also included which allow brighter images, less power consumption, lighter weight, and wider viewing angles.*
- *There are also pharmaceutical products that have improved absorption as they are reformulated with nanosized particles.*
- *They also involve nanostructured catalysts which make chemical manufacturing processes more efficient saving energy and decreasing waste products.*

In medicine and longevity, nanotechnology will play a vital role. People will become healthy when blood cell-sized devices will eradicate the pathogens by going directly into the human body. By using nanorobots full immersion in virtual reality and other advanced concepts will become possible. Macro scale objects can be created atom by atom basis by the so-called nanofabrication. Home appliances will download the products from the web and can serve as 3-D printers using this technology. Machines will be programmed by the physical atoms which would have their own algorithms or code.

With the help of nanotechnology invisibility cloaks, quantum computers and space elevators will become possible one day. There can be the reconstruction of entire bodies and brains at the atomic scale. This will lead to practical immortality. On the implications of nanotechnology, much debate has taken place. With a waste range of applications in medicine, engineering, electronics, and energy production, nanotech can produce new materials and devices. Many issues are raised by nanotechnologies such as concerns about the toxicity and environmental impact of nanomaterials including their influences on global economics. A discussion has been there among advocacy governments and groups due to these concerns. This debate is about the specific regulation of nanotechnology. Therefore, every industrial sector and healthcare field will be benefitted from nanotechnology. Through better ways of pollution control and more efficient use of resources, it also helps the environment and is eco-friendly.

Besides many risks are also posed by nanotech. The installation of proper regulatory oversight and collection of scientific information needed to resolve the ambiguities is required internationally. People will be assisted a lot by perceiving nanotech in a sober manner in a big picture that retains human value and quality of life. Nanomaterials and nanotechnologies have a very wide scope. Based on a large number of benefits, different organizations chose the area of research and its kind and applications. These advanced technology organizations are from different regions. Five market sectors have been identified by NAMI whose overloading objective is to commercialize to give an advantage to the PRD region.

www.ingramcontent.com/pod-product-compliance
Ingram Content Group UK Ltd.
Pitfield, Milton Keynes, MK11 3LW, UK
UKHW021921190726
13853UKWH00002B/771

9 798888 837030